**Y0-DKO-685**

# Dedication

*To the thousands of volunteers Who put their belief in action And quietly helped to comfort So many in need*

*Yet such is oft the course of the deeds that move the wheels of the world: small hands do them because they must, while the eyes of the great are elsewhere.*
*from The Fellowship of the Ring by J.R.R. Tolkien*

# CARING AND SHARING
## The History of Presbyterian Homes

Neil G. Gussman

All rights reserved. No part of this book may be reproduced in any form or by any means, without permission in writing from the author and Presbyterian Homes, Inc.

Address inquiries to:
Presbyterian Homes, Inc.
Administrative Office
1217 Slate Hill Road
Camp Hill, PA 17011

ISBN 0-9616428-0-7

Copyright © 1986
by Presbyterian Homes, Inc.
Printed in the United States of America

# Table of Contents

Caring and Sharing: A History of Presbyterian Homes
by Neil G. Gussman

## Acknowledgements

Most of the credit for the information in this book goes to the administrative staff at Presbyterian Homes, Inc., office in Camp Hill. They keep every manner of old documents in their files and were never too busy to answer questions, transcribe interviews, or just talk about their work. Special thanks are due to Lynn Christine, who knows where almost anything can be found, and to Romayne Bailey, who found many items I missed in the minutes of the Board of Trustee's meetings.

I also want to thank Dr. Michael Barton who got me started on this project and directed me to the best research material; Dr. Elizabeth Winston who showed me I could assemble all the parts and make a coherent whole; and my wife, Ida, who kept the rest of my life in perspective throughout the project.

Special thanks are due to Mr. William T. Swaim, Jr. who gave me hundreds of pages of documents on the corporation; John D. Killian, Esq., who gave me much information about Mr. Swaim; and many others who gave much time and effort helping with both research and revision of the manuscript.

## On Various Titles

As events transpire in this history of Presbyterian Homes, Inc., titles change. This reflects the times as well as increasing responsibilities of the various jobs. For instance, the men and women responsible for running individual homes started off with the titles Steward and Matron. Later, the same folks were called supervisors. Today these men and women are called administrators. The people living in the Homes were first referred to as guests. The change to residents more exactly expresses their place in the Homes. In all cases I used the proper title for the time I was describing.

Some of the titles change for the same person in the same job over time. The chief executive has held the title

Executive Secretary, Administrator, Executive Vice President, then most recently President and Chief Executive Officer. Although it is confusing, this paralleled the growth of the organization.

The name of the corporation began as Presbyterian Home of Central Pennsylvania; changed to Presbyterian Homes of Central Pennsylvania, then, in 1975, became, Presbyterian Homes, Inc. In this volume, the reference will be to the name current during the year I am describing when I use the full name. In places where the full name is particularly awkward, I will use "Homes" to refer to the corporation and "home" in subsequent references to a particular home within the corporation. Again, I will follow the current practice at the time it was in use.

## A Word on Leadership

For those who understand the intricacies of boards of directors, they may feel I have given undue place to the chief executives of Presbyterian Homes, Inc., in writing this history. The chief executive is, of course, beneath the board of directors and his principal duty is to carry out their policies. But the chief executive manages all the assets of a corporation from day to day and he is the one who makes the corporation go.

This distinction made, it is the drive, the energy, and the vision of the executive that moves any organization forward. If the executive seems to receive undue credit, he would receive an equal share of the blame for failure—were failure the stuff of this history.

The two men who have served Presbyterian Homes, Inc., as executive of the board for the past 52 years show, more than anything else, the wisdom of the trustees who appointed them and continued them in office. It is further to the board's credit that both men, William T. Swaim, Jr., and Albert L. Schartner, have made Presbyterian Homes, Inc., their lifes' work. Both men were and are experts in their fields and could have commanded higher salaries and benefits elsewhere. Their loyalty also speaks well for the board.

This brief volume will give the reader a chronicle of the people and the events that brought Presbyterian Homes,

Inc., from their humble beginnings to their present place as a major provider of care and housing for the aging in Pennsylvania and in neighboring states.

# Notes on Sources

The information contained in this book comes primarily from the files of Presbyterian Homes, Inc., and from the minutes of their board of trustees meetings, and from the minutes of the meetings of the committees of the board of trustees.

Information attributed directly to William T. Swaim, Jr., to Albert L. Schartner, and to other present and past members of the staff and board of Presbyterian Homes, Inc., came from personal interviews. Notes from the interviews are kept by the author. Tapes of the interviews with Swaim, and magnetic files of transcripts of those tapes are stored in the offices of Presbyterian Homes, Inc.

All publications of the corporation referred to in this book are on file at the offices of Presbyterian Homes, Inc., in Camp Hill, Pennsylvania. Some of the information about Swaim came from the files of John Killian, esq., the corporation's attorney, and a friend of Mr. Swaim's.

Any information not from the sources listed above is attributed at it's mention in the text.

# Preface

The development of Presbyterian Homes, Inc. is a thrilling story to behold. It demonstrates, first of all, the difference that can be made when Christians give their care and concern to the needs of others. It illustrates how, beginning with a vision of a few persons, others can catch that same vision until there are a multitude who are willing to give of their time, talents and energies to make a dream become a reality. It is often said that an organization is but the lengthened shadow of one or two who have given to it their lives. A reading of the story of Presbyterian Homes, Inc. makes apparent how this has been true from the very beginning. There is no way to measure the comfort and help that has been received by those who have been fortunate enough to be the constituency of this organization. The fact that many in their retirement years have found a place where they have received not only care but dignity is a wonderful testimony to what has been accomplished. Yet, those who have also contributed to make this possible have also greatly benefited by knowing that God has also used their lives to establish an organization which will continue to provide for the needs of others after they have themselves departed. At a time when so much of the world's resources are being used for those things which destroy, it is wonderful to behold that which touches the lives of others for good and in many ways demonstrates the presence of Almighty God. Presbyterian Homes, Inc. represents the very best and gives us a lasting example of what faith and compassion for our fellow human beings can accomplish.

The Rev. William G. Rusch, Ph.D.
Synod Executive
Synod of The Trinity

# 1

# The First Committees

*What we look for does not come to pass. God finds a way
for what none foresaw.* — Euripides

During the summer of 1920, a young widow returned
home to Mount Carmel with three young children. Her
husband had died in an influenza epidemic in Dallas, Texas,
a short time before the mother and her children returned
to Pennsylvania. She joined the First Presbyterian Church
of Mount Carmel, where J. Harold Wolf was the pastor.
While in Texas, she had converted from Roman Catholicism
to the Presbyterian Church. Her family in Mount Carmel
were all Roman Catholics.

In private conferences at the church, Wolf found the
woman was nearly broke, but willing to work. She wanted
to find a temporary home for her children so she could get
a regular job and begin to support them. Because she had
converted, her family would not help to care for her children.

Wolf first tried to get the children a home at the Presbyterian Orphanage in Philadelphia. He found that, since the
orphanage was a separate ministry from the church and
supported by Philadelphia Presbytery, they took care of
needs in their own area first. The superintendent of the
orphanage agreed to care for the two oldest children, but
the arrangement did not meet the mother's need. The
problem was her youngest child.

When the arrangements failed, the young widow returned
to Dallas. Whether her late husband's family helped the
young widow or not, we have no record. But she had an
effect on Wolf that lasted for the rest of his life. The

1

immediate problem was gone, but the need remained. Wolf investigated further and found the following:

The Presbyterians had fewer cases of needy children than other denominations, but did not have facilities adequate for their own small need. So needy children from Presbyterian churches were housed in orphanages sponsored by other denominations.

Many Presbyterians were giving large amounts of money to support care for children done by other denominations, since their own church was not involved in that work.

Because the denomination lacked facilities, they could not respond to urgent needs.

Armed with his general findings and the case from his own congregation, Wolf set up a committee in his own church to find a way to start an orphanage. On September 28, 1920, shortly after the young widow returned to Dallas, Wolf addressed a meeting of Northumberland Presbytery. He convinced the presbytery leaders to back his proposed Presbyterian orphanage.

The presbytery said they could raise money for the project. Mrs. Jane Harrison, a member of Lewisburg Presbyterian Church, offered to donate land for the project. But progress was slow.

Northumberland Presbytery thought building and operating a home was too much for the presbytery to handle alone. So Wolf set about involving other presbyteries in the project. And the work dragged on.

On June 10, 1923, the Synod of Pennsylvania met in Harrisburg to consider a proposal that all the presbyteries in the Synod work together to establish an orphanage. The Synod voted against the project, in part because Presbyterians in and around Philadelphia already had institutions of their own. Though the Synod would not fund a home, they recommended that neighboring Presbyteries organize to form a home. The Synod did not limit the scope of the work to either children or to the aging. By 1925 the committee represented seven presbyteries. Five of them—Northumberland, Lackawanna, Lehigh, Carlisle, and Westminster—would charter Presbyterian Home of Central Pennsylvania two years later. Clarion, the sixth, would drop out of the committee then reconsider and join Presbyterian Home of Central Pennsylvania in 1931. The seventh, Huntingdon Presbytery, dropped out of the proposed corporation after they were given a home with an endowment to operate it within their own presbytery.

Other problems came with the increasing size of the committee. The delegation from Carlisle had already formed their own corporation called Presbyterian Home for the Aged. The Carlisle group included a man named Walter Stuart who had long hoped to see a Presbyterian home for the aging. Wolf still favored a children's home, as did members of the other cooperating Presbyteries. Dr. W. M. Workman of Mount Joy, one of the original trustees, was most interested in a convalescent home. Despite the differing opinions of the greatest need, the work went forward.

The committee had three properties to choose from to start the home. The Harrison Farm in Lewisburg; a 100-acre farm in Shade Gap offered by J. W. Harper; and the Parker Farm in Newville, Cumberland County. Each of the properties was an "out in the country" location which followed the practice and thinking of the time on where the aging should live. Of the three properties, the Parker Farm needed least development. It also promised the most financial support since Carlisle Presbytery had already incorporated this property as a home for the aging on its own. The committee decided to accept the Parker Farm.

The remaining five Presbyteries—Carlisle, Lehigh, Lackawanna, Northumberland, and Westminster—met again and decided to start a home for aging ladies. The Carlisle group had already begun to build a home for the aging so this ministry promised the widest initial support. They also decided to leave their options open. The charter they eventually adopted stated that the corporation was also formed to care for dependent children and for convalescent children, but the initial work would be a home for the aging on the Parker Farm in Newville.

Early in 1925, Carlisle Presbytery formed a corporation on their own to begin a home for the aging. Spring meetings between the other Presbyteries and the Carlisle group brought agreement that all the interested Presbyteries should cooperate on the project. The joint venture meant that the Carlisle corporation called Presbyterian Home for the Aging must be dissolved so the Parker Farm could be donated to the new, larger corporation.

On June 15, 1925, Presbyterian Home for the Aging was dissolved and the farm deeded back to Mrs. Parker. She then turned the property over to the trustees of the new corporation, which would eventually be called Presbyterian Home of Central Pennsylvania. Her price for the property was one dollar. The original property included a brick farmhouse and 91 acres of land.

With the Parker Farm and five cooperating presbyteries, the new organization needed a charter and the money to renovate the Parker Farm. They raised the money through various means and the first home opened in September of 1928.

Mrs. Parker gave more property to Presbyterian Home of Central Pennsylvania in the years that followed. In 1931 she gave the corporation 93 acres adjoining the original farm in return for a life annuity of $202.50 per year. She returned the annuity to the home as a contribution each year until her death. In 1933 she sold the house at 602 N. Hanover Street in Carlisle, which she had built as an orphanage 31 years before, to the corporation. Her price was one gold dollar. The balance of her estate of nearly $200,000 was held in trust for the general purposes of the corporation and eventually was turned over to the Homes completely after her son Lewis died in 1956.

Mrs. Parker's concern for the aging set the direction for the new corporation. Her large and continued gifts to the corporation sustained its work through the worst years of the depression.

Residents enjoy sleigh ride.

Ellen A. Parker

# 2

# Ellen Ard Parker

*Too much happens. . .Man performs, engenders so much more than he can or should have to bear. That's how he finds out he can bear anything.* —William Faulkner

In 1917, Mrs. Ellen A. Parker returned from a two year convalescence in Alabama to her home in Carlisle and to her home church—the Second Presbyterian Church of Carlisle. She was 65- years-old and very tired. Two years before she had closed an orphanage that she had built and had run almost entirely on her own for four years. She housed 20 young orphans in a home at 602 North Hanover Street in Carlisle, the same building that is now Carlisle Presbyterian Home. Mrs. Parker was a woman of property and wealth and had been so for most of her life. She was known for her beauty as a young woman. She could have lived life in all the luxury that her time had to offer, but she spent her life caring for children and caring for the elderly and denying herself comfort for the sake of others.

From the record we have of her life, Ellen Parker's works of charity toward others seem to grow from a succession of personal tragedies. Like her ill-fated attempt to run an orphanage on her own in the seventh decade of her life, most of the great joys of Mrs. Parker's life melted into sadness. But each setback brought her to some new act of selflessness. Her final act of charity, giving all of her property to the ministry of Presbyterian Homes, Inc., has grown beyond all the hopes she had—and makes a fitting tribute to a life lived for others.

Ellen Hoover was born in Lewistown, Pennsylvania, on July 20, 1852. She was the daughter of Dr. and Mrs. Lewis

Hoover. Dr. Hoover practiced medicine in Lewistown until he died at age 40. That was in 1853 when his daughter Ellen was one-year-old. Ellen's mother, Mary McCoy Hoover, cared for her children alone for the next ten years.

Ellen's mother met and married a new husband during the Civil War. Though it's not clear how wealthy Ellen's new father was at the time they married, Captain Cyrus K. Mark of the Union Army became a captain of industry after his war service ended. Shortly after Captain Mark and Mrs. Hoover were married, Mark adopted Ellen and she was sent to an exclusive girl's school in Birmingham, Pennsylvania, during the last year of the war. The school Ellen attended was known as Mountain Seminary in 1865. The name was later changed to the Grier School for Girls.

After the war Captain Mark worked in Lebanon, Pennsylvania, as an iron manufacturer, then moved to Pine Grove Furnace, 12 miles south of Newville, to take a job as manager of the South Mountain Iron Ore Company.

Ellen was a society woman in her early 20s. She and her best friend Amelia Given were known as "the blonde and brunette beauties." Ellen was called the "Belle of Cumberland Valley." Life, for Ellen, seemed a continuous round of parties and social events. In 1872, when Ellen was 20 years old, she married her best friend's brother, Samuel Given.

The Given family was part of the same social set as the Marks. Robert Given, Samuel's father, owned a paper mill in Mount Holly Springs. The same year Ellen and Samuel were married, Samuel Given died of tuberculosis ("consumption" in the records). Samuel was one of four children of the Given family to die of tuberculosis between 1870 and 1872. He was 24-years-old. Ellen, now a widow in her early 20s, moved back to her family home. She remained a widow for four years.

The Mark family then moved to Carlisle where Ellen met and married William Henderson Parker. Mrs. Parker is named on the records of the Second Presbyterian Church of Carlisle as a new member on November 25, 1876, shortly after her marriage. Parker was a successful herdsman. He took Ellen west to Wyoming with him where they lived for the next several years. They followed the cattle drives to market in a pony wagon and, according to one story told by a friend, the Parkers nearly drowned while fording the North Platte River on one of the cattle drives.

In the early 1880s Parker sold his 2,000 acres of ranch land in Wyoming and Nebraska. When they returned to Carlisle, in 1884, the Parker's bought a spacious house at 315 N. Market Street in Carlisle and a 258-acre farm near Newville. That same year, 1884, William Parker made out his Last Will and Testament. It would be executed less than two years later.

On February 7, 1886, William Henderson Parker died after an illness lasting several months. Whether tuberculosis claimed Mrs. Parker's second husband is not recorded. Whatever the cause, Mrs. Parker watched at bedside for months while her second husband died, just as she had her first husband 14 years before. Mrs. Parker remained a widow for the rest of her life. Whether she had any suitors or not would be speculation. What is clear is Mrs. Parker's devotion to the memory of her second husband. Her gift of the first home and farm to Presbyterian Home of Central Pennsylvania was made in his name and in his memory.

The records at Second Presbyterian Church do not record William Henderson Parker as a member of the church, but his death is entered in the record with the phrase "cut off in the prime of life." He was buried in Ashland Cemetery, Carlisle, where Ellen would also be interred almost 50 years later.

The simple will that Mr. Parker wrote in 1884 left $6,000 to each of his brothers and the balance of his estate to his wife. The will included a provision to divide the estate among any children the couple would have in the future, a future that must have looked very bright in 1884. The couple was childless.

Ellen's parents came to live with her soon after William Parker died. Captain Mark died shortly after they moved to the Parker Home, so Ellen and her mother, both widows, shared the home Ellen's late husband provided for them.

Mrs. Parker worked to provide care for orphaned children in her community during the years that followed. Although her interest was primarily in care for children for the rest of her life, her mother often talked about homes for aging women who had no family. "It's nice they give those ladies a home," Mrs. Mark would say. According to Bill Swaim, some specific concerns Mrs. Parker had for the aging grew from the experience of caring for her own mother. Before Mrs. Mark died she was often very cold. Ellen Parker piled blankets on her mother and kept the fire in the house hot, but she could not keep her mother warm enough. Mrs. Parker would later insist that the temperature always be kept very warm in the homes as a result of her mother's discomfort at a time when Swaim remembers visiting Mrs. Parker in her own very cold house. Even in her 80s, Mrs. Parker denied herself central heat yet she demanded that the homes be kept very warm. During these same years, she was turning over large gifts to the work of Presbyterian Home of Central Pennsylvania.

Mrs. Parker's concern for orphans went beyond donating her time and her money. On June 25, 1890, she presented a child for baptism in the Second Presbyterian Church. She had taken the boy in as a foster child and later adopted him. He was born September 6, 1888. The boy was baptised William Lewis Parker, though in later life he went by his middle name alone.

Mrs. Parker raised Lewis while she cared for her aging mother. Though the record of Lewis Parker's life is more sketchy than that of his mother, it's clear he spent most of his life as a railroad worker living in the Southern states. He died in McAllen, Texas, in 1956 at age 68. Though he was not directly involved with the work of the Home, he lived in a small farmhouse on the Parker Farm when he was in Pennsylvania.

In 1900 Mrs. Parker, now in her late forties and caring for her widowed mother and a 12-year-old son, started planning and building a home for orphaned children at 602 N. Hanover Street, the building which is now Carlisle Presbyterian Home. The home was opened and dedicated in 1911 housing 20 children. For four years following the opening of the home, Mrs. Parker lived in and ran the home for orphaned children.

In 1915 Ellen Parker was 63 years old and running the

orphanage largely on her own. Her health failed. She closed the home and moved to Alabama for two years to rest. In 1917 she returned to Carlisle and moved back into the home she and her husband first lived in 30 years before.

From this point, Mrs. Parker's biography winds together with Walter Stuart, the Rev. Glenn Shafer and the beginning of Presbyterian Home of Central Pennsylvania.

Walter Stuart, a Carlisle banker and a member of Second Presbyterian Church, had seen a need for many years for a Presbyterian home for the aging. The Rev. Glenn Shafer was elected pastor of Second Presbyterian Church in 1917, the same year Mrs. Parker returned from Alabama. Shafer shared Stuart's concern. The two men would work more and more closely with Mrs. Parker in the coming years as the work of a Presbyterian home began to take shape. But in 1917 neither man had an answer to the question of how to begin such a large work.

Soon after her return, Mrs. Parker went to her minister, the Rev. Glenn Shafer, for advice about writing her will. Shafer sent her to Stuart who seems to have convinced her to set aside part of her estate for the care of aging Presbyterians.

As a result of Stuart's advice, and with help from Shafer and other like-thinking members of Carlisle Presbytery, Mrs. Parker donated the Parker Farm as the basis of a corporation called "Presbyterian Home for the Aged." The corporation was chartered in the Court of Cumberland County on March 3, 1925. Why the corporation was formed seven years after the first conversations that Stuart, Shafer, and Mrs. Parker had about the ministry is not clear from the records. It seems the Carlisle group, like Wolf's groups in Mount Carmel, found the business of beginning a new non-profit corporation where none existed before more work than anyone expected.

The last ten years of Mrs. Parker's life, until her death on April 8, 1935, was spent largely on work for the Homes. She deeded the Parker Farm in Newville to the new corporation, but the corporation dissolved and the farm was deeded back to her on June 15th of 1925.

At the same time Mrs. Parker, Mr. Stuart, Dr. Shafer, and

the others that formed the new corporation were at work in Carlisle, other Presbyterians were working, from Wolf's efforts, to form a Presbyterian benevolent work for a wider area in Central Pennsylvania. By 1927, the two groups became one. Wolf's committees from the other four Presbyteries and the men and women of Carlisle Presbytery agreed on the site of the new home, the name of the new corporation, and the type of care they would begin providing.

The new corporation was chartered in the Court of Common Pleas of Cumberland County in 1927. Because the charter included every kind of care that each of the founders wanted to provide, and because it restricted that care to "White Presbyterians," the charter was completely rewritten in 1962 to remove the restrictive language. With all its flaws, the first charter gave the corporation a legal basis. Work began to renovate the Parker Home into a home for the aging at the beginning of the following year.

Before the first guest arrives, we should define the kind of home the founders opened. Though nursing care makes up the greater share of the care provided by Presbyterian Homes, Inc., today, Presbyterian Home of Central Pennsylvania gave its guests a different sort of care. It was not until 1970 that the Home's ministry included nursing care. For the first forty years the corporation provided shelter for women who needed a place to live and were active and well. The first ten Presbyterian Homes were called Residential Homes.

First Residents of the Parker Home.

Residents enjoy the fellowship of a meal.

# 3

# Homes Alone

*Be Obscure Clearly.* —Casey Stengel

When most people think of homes for the aging, they think of nursing homes. Nursing homes, those that provide round the clock medical care for their patients, make up the vast majority of homes in this country. In the last fifteen years, Presbyterian Homes, Inc., has joined the rest of the care providers in this nation in making nursing care the majority of its work.

But it was not always so. For the first 40 years of its history, Presbyterian Homes, Inc., provided a fast disappearing type of care known as residential care, an intermediate level between independent living and nursing care.(*)

The most common, whether in or out of an institution of any kind, is independent living. Independent living is the way most of us live. Whether in apartments, condominiums, or private residences, independent living is the preferred and most common lifestyle for everyone in the United States, including those of retirement age.

At the other end of the scale is nursing care. Nursing care provides the services necessary to sustain the life of those who can no longer care for themselves and require professional nursing services. When eating, taking routine medication, and even bathing become tasks too great for one person or for the family, the nursing home provides those services.

In between independent living and nursing care is residential care. The men and women living in residential care facilities have their own rooms. They need little or no help

15

getting around and are largely self sufficient. Persons living in residential care homes eat their meals together in a common dining room. The residents of these homes are usually women who were living alone before they entered the home.

For an older person living alone, cooking meals and performing heavy housekeeping chores can be extremely taxing. Residential care relieves them of these responsibilities while affording them a large measure of independence. Since all of the residential homes except the first and the third had downtown addresses, the residents have many activities open to them. Shopping, movies, church, and community activities are all close by.

The majority of the Home's history until 1970 is a story of residential care. Only one new residential home has opened in the last decade, and that, The Steward Home at Oxford Manor, is actually a wing of a larger nursing facility.

That residential facilities were the only care offered by the Homes for 40 years, could seem strange to anyone looking at the present list of the homes that comprise Presbyterian Homes, Inc. Today nursing care and Independent Living (including separately incorporated apartments) make up more than 80 percent of the facilities operated. By budget, by sheer numbers of residents, by personnel, and by any other criteria, nursing homes dominate the ministry of Presbyterian Homes, Inc. The changeover was rapid. Starting in 1972 with Forest Park Health Center, nursing homes were bought and built at a rate of one every two years through 1985.

Several factors contributed to the shift in direction. The most obvious was the change in the leadership of the corporation in late 1969. In December of that year, Bill Swaim retired after nearly 30 years as full-time administrator of the corporation and six additional years as part time administrator that preceded his full-time position. During the last five years of Swaim's tenure, beginning in 1965, President Johnson's Great Society legislation changed federal policy. Medicare and Medicaid would pay for nursing care but would not pay for residential care. Advances in medical technology lengthened the life span and dramatically increased the size of the elderly population. Older persons lived at home longer and were more likely to need nursing care when they had to leave their homes.

The Parker Home opened before Social Security, before penicillin, before effective cancer treatment, long before heart surgery of any kind, in short, before advances in medicine and advances in social legislation raised the quality of life for the aging.

Many of the women who would have entered residential homes were now living in apartments designed for the elderly. After World War II, rapid advances in medical care were so common they could be taken almost for granted. As medical science advanced, the life span of Americans increased. And that life span was not only longer but healthier. Older Americans moved to apartments and condominiums at retirement.

In the 1970s, home health care services began to bring routine medical care into private homes. Activity centers for the aging and "meals on wheels" allowed those who would have been candidates for residential care in the decades past to live at home longer.

Longer life spans increase the need for nursing care. The shift to nursing care is a natural change of direction to meet the changing needs of the people they serve. Up to that point in the history of the corporation, we will be talking about residential homes with private bedrooms, common parlors, communal dining, and minimal medical care.

(*) That residential care is "fast disappearing" is primarily due to its cost. To provide residential care in modern times means running a home conforming to nearly all the federal and state guidelines for nursing care, yet providing no medical care. Currently, residential care costs about $31 per day or more than 75% of the cost of nursing care. Unlike nursing care, residential care is not eligible for Medicare or Medicaid reimbursement.

Since residential care receives no subsidy, only those older persons who can afford its high cost, or those whom the Presbyterian Homes, Inc., benevolent funds can support, live in this type of home. Presbyterian Homes,

Inc., will not disclose the names of those receiving benevolent care to protect the privacy of both the recipients and of the men and women who are paying for their own care. Benevolent care for residential care homes has consistently used nearly $300,000 per year of the benevolent care budget of Presbyterian Homes, Inc., during the 1980s.

The Parker Home

# 4

# The Parker Home

*Success is a journey, not a destination.* —Ben Sweetland

The Parker Home opened on September 17, 1928, with grand plans and lots of financial trouble—$8,000 in debt with only the generosity of the constituent churches to count on to pay off their indebtedness. The architectural firm of Lawrie and Green planned the renovation of the Parker Farmhouse in 1927. The changes, costing $10,000 made the home ready for nine guests. The trustees approved the changes and the work went ahead without full funding. The corporation eventually got an $8,500 line of credit, of which it used $8,000. But the financing was not guaranteed quickly.

In fact, George Hackett of Sunbury, one of the original trustees, attended one of the preliminary meetings for the opening of The Parker Home with five $1,000 government bonds in his pocket to offer as collateral—just in case the corporation couldn't borrow the money it needed to open the first home. Hackett also loaned the corporation $1,500 for the purchase of 80 sheep. The plan was that the sheep should supplement the income of the home. The plans were well-meant, but farm commodity prices collapsed with the rest of the economy the following year. The sheep were part of the Parker Farm through 1962, and lost more money for the home than they made.

The nine original guests moved in almost immediately, as did the first matron of the home, Mrs. Mary Hartzell. She served for one year, but was dismissed after a disagreement with the trustees concerning the food she served to the guests. Mr. and Mrs. Kerr Lott were then hired to run the home. Mr. Lott served as steward of the farm, Mrs. Lott as the matron.

Within a month after the opening day of the first home, the trustees called their architectural firm again to design a larger home to be built on the Parker Farm. At the board meeting held on October 22, 1929, Mr. Lawrie presented sketches and suggestions for the building of a cottage to house 20 additional guests. The trustees adopted the building plan as presented. On January 20 of the following year, Mr. Green came to the meeting with plans for a larger building. At the March meeting of the executive committee, the plans for the smaller building were dropped, the plans for the larger were adopted, but the expansion was never carried out. The proposed smaller building, Cottage "A," would have cost $40,000. The larger building, Cottage "B," would cost $75,000. At the same meeting during which the plans for the larger building were adopted, the balance in the operating budget of the treasury was $207.81 with an additional $47.15 in the sheep fund.

On Dedication Day for The Parker Home, October 4, 1928, the corporation hired a full-time field representative: the Rev. F. E. Taylor. During his tenure, he traveled to churches throughout the five presbyteries (six in 1931 when Clarion Presbytery joined the corporation) telling church members, women's groups, and anyone else who would listen about the work of the home. Taylor founded both the Women's Auxiliary and the Harvest Home Day gathering. He conducted the first Mother's Day appeals for contributions. The accounts of his work in the minutes of the board show devotion to his work, but raising money for a new benevolent work in the midst of the Depression showed few results. Despite Taylor's efforts—visiting, writing letters to wealthy church members, organizing fund raising activities, and the like, the original $8,000 debt remained on the books for the first 4 1/2 years the corporation was in operation. More than half of the original debt was paid off in October of 1931 by funds left by two guests who died earlier in that year. The remainder of the original debt was paid in 1933 from a bequest made to the home from an estate in York.

In that same year, Taylor's job was discontinued. Taylor's salary of $2,500 per year was the largest single item in the budget until 1933 when he was put on part-time work by the board of trustees. His salary, without expenses, represented more than 25 percent of the budget throughout the period he worked full time. Taylor's services were terminated with regret both by the board and by Taylor, but the budget had to be cut.

The Women's Auxiliary, as noted above, was organized by Taylor. The first meeting was held in 1929 at the home of Miss Anne McCormick of Pine Street Presbyterian Church in Harrisburg. The auxiliary quickly got involved with the work of the homes and raised money for special needs. The history of the auxiliary has been one of finding money to buy the things the treasury could not stretch to cover.

One of the first projects the auxiliary got involved with was buying an electric refrigerator for The Parker Home. Electric refrigerators were not the rule in private residences, but their value was obvious for institutions. The auxiliary raised $175 toward a new refrigerator and offered it to the board on April 29, 1930. The board declined the offer since the treasury balance at the time of the meeting was only $200. By June of the following year, the auxiliary raised the entire price of the refrigerator and had it installed in The Parker Home.

So by 1933, The Parker Home and Presbyterian Home of Central Pennsylvania were out of debt and operating in the black. That same year, Mrs. Parker donated the orphanage she had run two decades earlier. Her price was one gold dollar. That gold dollar was donated to the corporation and paid to Mrs. Parker by George Hackett. The corporation was now ready for its first expansion. A new trustee joined the board in that year. He was 27-years-old, the second son of an Evangelical preacher, and the new pastor of Big Spring Presbyterian Church in Newville. This new board member quickly got involved with the day-to-day operation of the Parker Home, as well as with the renovations just beginning at the second home in Carlisle which Mrs. Parker had recently donated to the corporation. Within a year this new board member, William T. Swaim, Jr., became the executive secretary of the board as well as the de facto administrator of the corporation. His enthusiasm for the work of administration seemed boundless from the beginning. It remained so for the 36 years that followed until his retirement and continues to the present time.

William T. Swaim, Jr.

# 5

# The Swaim Years

*If you want to know what a man is, place him in authority.*
—A Yugoslav Proverb

On May 2, 1933, President of the Board of Trustees Harry Keeny announced that Carlisle Presbytery had elected the Rev. William T. Swaim, Jr., pastor of the Big Spring Presbyterian Church in Newville, as a trustee of the Home, in the place made vacant by the Rev. F. T. Wheeler.

With this announcement Bill Swaim began more than 36 years of service to Presbyterian Homes, Inc. The young minister from the Texas panhandle had recently been elected pastor of the Newville congregation after serving for a short time as assistant pastor of the Pine Street Presbyterian Church in Harrisburg.

Swaim was intrigued by the work of the Home from the beginning. Fourteen days after Swaim was named to fill the Rev. Wheeler's seat on the board of trustees, Wheeler died and Swaim was given a seat on the executive committee of the board.

In June, Swaim was made treasurer of the revolving fund which paid the operating bills for the Parker Farm. In July, Swaim was made purchasing agent for the farm for the coming winter. On February 5, 1934, Swaim was named acting secretary of the executive committee in place of the Rev. T. Edwin Redding. Redding had increasing responsibilities as assistant pastor of the First Presbyterian Church of Lancaster. The pastor of First Presbyterian, the Rev. Walter Edge, another trustee of the Home, had been ill for more than a year, putting the responsibility of the pastorate

23

and the secretary's duties on Redding alone. The Rev. Edge died in the Spring of 1934.

On May 2, 1934, one year after Swaim was made a trustee, he was officially named secretary of the executive committee. On the same day Swaim's salary was raised from $50 per year to $10 per month. Later in the year, the offices of Executive Secretary and Swaim's present office as secretary of the executive committee were combined.

Swaim took on more and more responsibility for the operation of the homes each year, but his full-time job as administrator of the corporation would not begin until 1940.

Swaim's enthusiasm made him the logical choice for the job from the beginning, but the Depression was on and the young corporation spent a lot of time juggling accounts and borrowing money on short term notes to pay for operating expenses. The board dropped the salaries of the steward and the matron of the Parker Farm twice in the first year Swaim worked for the corporation. The board also terminated the Rev. Taylor, its part- time field representative, in 1935.

So Swaim had to wait until the board was sure they could afford a full-time administrator. Swaim was finally elected when the work of running three homes and building a fourth meant there was so much work they could no longer do without a full-time administrator.

Once elected, Swaim gave several reports in the first years of his full time work that justified the need for a full time administrator. These same reports would lead some of the trustees to push for an assistant administrator beginning in 1951. Swaim resisted the idea for several years. As the office ran smoothly and the corporation grew with an office staff consisting of Swaim and two secretaries, so the issue of the corporation's need for an assistant administrator waxed and waned through the 1950s and early 1960s.

In 1963 Swaim had surgery for a detached retina. His six week recuperation showed that the office could not, in fact, run without him. Then two years later, Swaim had ill-advised surgery on his hands that made driving, typing, and normal office chores laborious and painful. Six years before Swaim retired, slightly more than thirty years after he became secretary of the executive committee, the Rev. Albert Schartner left a pastorate of seven years to become Swaim's assistant.

Bill Swaim retired in December of 1969. All but the first of the ten original homes opened during the 36 years Bill Swaim served the corporation. During his tenure the direction of the corporation shifted from developing the Parker Farm as a center for both homes for the aging and homes for orphans to the "Small, Scattered, Home-Like Homes for the Aging" which were eventually located in five of the six cooperating Presbyteries. When Swaim was first elected secretary, The Parker Home in Newville housed eleven ladies on the Parker Farm. At his retirement the corporation housed more than 400 aging men and women in nine residential homes, a large apartment complex in downtown Harrisburg, and a mansion converted into apartments located in Oxford. (The Andrews Home in Newville, the third Presbyterian home, closed two years before Swaim's retirement.)

Swaim retired to live with his wife, Alice, in Presbyterian Apartments, the last building project completed during Swaim's tenure.

The Andrews Home

# 6

# Expansion in Depression

*The only question with wealth is what you do with it.*
— John D. Rockefeller, Jr.

The year 1933 opened with Presbyterian Home of Central Pennsylvania operating as it had for the five years since its beginning. The annual budget was less than $10,000 including salaries, maintenance, and office expenses. The largest item in the budget was the salary paid to a tireless fundraiser who worked through the worst years in the economic history of our country.

The annual budget in 1933 would have operated Presbyterian Homes, Inc., for just 3 hours and 11 minutes in 1983. But the small budget kept the corporation open and serving the aging until better times later in the decade.

The close management of the corporation is best illustrated by a three-month long debate that carried through the spring and summer meetings of the executive committee as recorded in the minutes of the committee. A summary of those proceedings follows:

When the April 1933 meeting of the executive committee of the board of trustees convened, one item of financial business was whether Mr. Lott, the steward (manager of the farm and buildings) for The Parker Home should be authorized to buy additional lambs for the growing flock at the farm in Newville. Also Mrs. Lott, matron of the home, was considering buying a brood of laying hens. Both matters were tabled for further study. Two months later, after consultation with the Cumberland County Office of Agriculture, Mr. Lott was authorized to buy ten more lambs

27

and Mrs. Lott was allowed to buy sixty chicks with which she could raise a brood of hens.

To finance the purchases, the contents of the cow fund ($117.04) were transferred to the fund for retiring the present debt on the sheep. Mr. Lott, according to the minutes of the June meeting, assured the trustees that the present cow was in good health and that another cow would be unnecessary in the "foreseeable future."

With ten more sheep, 60 new chicks, and a total operating budget of $9,550 (including salaries, food, office expenses, rents, and interest on debts), Presbyterian Home of Central Pennsylvania concluded their fifth year of operation with eleven elderly women as guests in the home and plans to open another home within a year.

Part of the reason the corporation needed contributions and often ran so close to zero in its operating account was the open-handed generosity of its fees for care. Miss Mary Horner filled the first vacancy in The Parker Home on January 18, 1929, at age 61. She entered the home paying the $600 fee set for admission for guests of her age group (ages 60-65 paid $600, 66-70 paid $500, over 70 at admission, was $400.). The admission fee contracted the corporation to provide residential care, an allowance, any hospitalization and nursing care the guest would need, and interment in the tradition of the church.

Mary Horner was a personal friend of Mrs. Parker and was, according to Bill Swaim, "an outstanding guest in every way." Miss Horner died August 13, 1948, after slightly more than 19 years as a guest at The Parker Home. Since the admission fee was the only fee, Miss Horner paid just nine cents per day for 19 years of room, board, and necessary medical care. The admission fees are different today—but men and women still enter residential care with even less than Mary Horner brought to the homes. (In fact, the net loss on residential care in the 1980s has exceeded a quarter of a million dollars each year.) From the beginning, the corporation was constituted to care for people with no one else to care for them, but providing this kind of benevolent care has strained the budget throughout most the history of the corporation.(*)

But the corporation continued to expand. As noted earlier, Mrs. Parker turned over the house she had built for an orphanage to the home for one gold dollar in 1933. The Parker Annex, as the home at 602 North Hanover Street was called, opened in January of 1934 and filled with guests almost immediately. The name of the home, The Parker Annex, indicates the direction of the trustees plans for the future of the corporation in 1934.

Mrs. Parker specified that the Parker Annex could be sold at any time the trustees deemed appropriate with the proceeds used to expand the facilities at the Parker Farm in Newville. The plans to build at the Parker Farm were still hanging on the wall in the Parker Home in 1934 and the trustees still thought of their homes as country homes for older women to live out their sunset years.

By the time The Parker Annex opened, Bill Swaim had become the *de facto* administrator of the corporation for the board of trustees. He handled interviews with prospective employees and brought prospective residents to see the two homes when they were applying for admission. Applicants met the executive committee of the board prior to admission, but Swaim conducted the tours. Soon after Swaim began conducting the tours, he realized that most of the residents wanted to live in town. The facts of these women's lives just did not match up with the stereotypes. They wanted to live near shopping and theaters and libraries and church—near life in the community.

In fact, according to Swaim, his initial practice for prospective guests at The Parker Home was to meet them in Carlisle, give them a tour of The Parker Annex when they were in town, then drive out to the farm. The majority of the guests- elect, on seeing the home in Carlisle, wanted to live there, not out on the farm. Swaim soon stopped the complimentary tours to avoid making prospective farm guests wish to live elsewhere before they were admitted. This experience jelled the corporate policy of opening "Small, Scattered, Home-Like, Homes for the Aging" that would guide the policy and expansion of Presbyterian Home of Central Pennsylvania through the 1950s and 1960s. Despite the evidence of the preferences of the guests, the board was not entirely convinced that future homes should be located in or near the center of towns and cities. Five years later, Swaim would find, to his surprise and dismay, that he could not assume a majority of the board was convinced of the facts he knew so well.

The next home to open, like the first two homes, was the gift of a widow who was the only surviving member of her immediate family. The building was a house known in Newville as "Tarry-A- While." The property was bequeathed to Carlisle Presbytery with a $5,000 endowment fund to be used for maintenance of the property. Since the will did not restrict the use or the guestship of the home to Carlisle Presbytery, the presbytery turned over the property and the endowment to Presbyterian Home of Central Pennsylvania for stewardship of the gift. The will stipulated that the home be used for at least 25 years. The Andrews Annex, as it was named, (later The Andrews Home) was open for 30 years until government regulations on access and the size of hallways made its continued use impossible in 1968.

The home was given by Mrs. Helen McCune Andrews, a long-time member of Big Spring Presbyterian Church in Newville where Bill Swaim served as pastor. The gift was a memorial to Mrs. Andrews' husband and to her daughter. Mr. James K. Andrews died in 1930. Their daughter, Marie Andrews Chapman, died in 1926. The home was built in 1906 and used as a summer home by the Andrews family. They lived in New York City during the fall and winter months and returned to Newville late in the spring.

The new home was renovated for just over $4,000 and opened in 1938. The original renovations made seven single rooms and two double rooms for a total of eleven guests.

By 1941, the double rooms became single rooms. The trustees made it a matter of policy that two guests would not have to share a room. Bill Swaim said throughout his tenure as administrator that no room was big enough for two guests and held to the policy of single occupancy in residential rooms throughout his tenure. The policy is the same today in the residential homes.

Like the corporation's policy of locating homes in towns and cities as opposed to the "Out in the Country" setting, stipulating single occupancy went against the practice of the time and was motivated by the desires of their guests. One guest drew a chalk line on the floor in the middle of a double room to show how she felt about the shared living space arrangement.

By 1938, the corporation operated three homes. The expansion meant progress, but the corporation was still quite young and plagued by growing pains. In 1934, the first president of the women's auxiliary resigned over a disagreement with Mrs. Parker. Miss Anne McCormick, president of the auxiliary, wanted The Parker Home to have a dispensary and was willing to pay for its construction. When Mrs. Parker blocked the plans, Miss McCormick left the auxiliary, although in later years endowments left by Miss McCormick continued to benefit the work of the Homes. These were not the only disputes.

(*)New guests were expected to turn over all of their assets to the corporation as part of their entry into the home. They received interest payments on the excess monies over the admission fee. Throughout the history of the corporation, if a prospective guest did not have the admission fee, they would be admitted in any case. Bill Swaim argued for several years that the admission fee should be abolished for just that reason—anyone could be admitted as a guest with or without the fee. Whether Mary Horner paid any monies in excess of the entry fee is not a matter of record. Her case only serves to illustrate the care a guest could expect to receive if all the money she had was the entry fee, or less.

The Carlisle Home

# 7

# Growing Pains

*There is nothing more difficult to take in hand, more perilous to conduct, or more uncertain in its success, than to take the lead in the introduction of a new order of things.*
—Niccolo Machiavelli

As noted in the introduction to this section, Bill Swaim's ascendancy to full-time administrator of Presbyterian Home of Central Pennsylvania was a slow process made slower by the worst Depression in the history of the nation. Until 1940, his work at the homes was part-time. Swaim's primary work was serving as pastor of Big Spring Presbyterian Church in Newville.

At the time Swaim began his pastoral duties and his work for Presbyterian Home of Central Pennsylvania, Mr. and Mrs. J. Kerr Lott were the steward and the matron at The Parker Home. Mr. Lott was an elder in Swaim's congregation.

In 1934, some of the guests in the home wrote to the trustees complaining about Mrs. Lott in lengthy detail. They levelled several specific charges against her which she was called in to answer. Mr. Lott was also accused of lack of industry in caring for the farm.

Swaim investigated the problems at length in the Fall and Winter of 1934 and wrote lengthy letters to the board and to individual trustees explaining the Lott's circumstances, its changed attitude, and the steps they were taking to correct the problems. Swaim investigated as administrator at the same time he was counseling the couple as their pastor. The end of Swaim's diplomatic balancing of pastoral and corporate duties was a one year grace period that saw the Lott's replaced at its end.

The following year, a dentist's wife who was serving as keywoman at The Parker Annex called Swaim at home to set up a conference. The purpose of the conference was to be threefold:

To set rules "to keep these old ladies in their place,"

To tell the staff "not to take anything off these old ladies,"

And to appoint herself and the matron as the Admissions Committee for their Home.

The demands, as Swaim recalls them, were all made over the telephone. His answer was returned the same way. Swaim dismissed the demands out of hand saying that a committee of that constituency would have no standing in Presbyterian Home of Central Pennsylvania. The corporation and the trustees have all of the power. The trustees have delegated all administrative responsibilities to the Executive.

Swaim's summary of the incident was brief, "She resigned and the Homes survived without her. Then the Board passed a motion that the Women's Auxiliary had no power over policies or personnel."

Trouble from the auxiliary, from the employees, or from the guests themselves was the exception rather than the rule throughout the history of the corporation, but with any new enterprise, many of the rules grew out of problems no one anticipated when the work began. The homes, as Swaim said, survived their growing pains and were ready to expand the work. Although the corporation had been in business for eight years by 1936, they had no regular mailing to the more than 400 constituent churches aside from Mother's Day contribution envelopes.

Three years before, in 1933, the Rev. F. E. Taylor left his work as a full-time fund raiser for the corporation. His absence left a large gap in the work of getting the word about the homes out to the constituent churches in the six presbyteries that made up Presbyterian Home of Central Pennsylvania. Swaim partially filled this need by giving talks and slide presentations to churches and church groups throughout the several presbyteries. But Swaim couldn't be everywhere at once. To spread the word about the homes *The Newville Homes News* (now *The Presbyterian Homes News*) was created.

The News

# 8

# "The Newville Home News"

*News is the first rough draft of history.* —Ben Bradlee

In 1936, Bill Swaim put together a four-page, 5 1/2 by 8-inch newsletter called *The Newville Home News.* The little publication's first printing of 5,000 copies was mailed to key persons involved in the ministry of the homes in churches throughout the six constituent Presbyteries. That first issue heralded the coming Harvest Home Day on the front page, with details and other news about the homes on the second and third pages. The back page listed all 21 guests with their home church, their presbytery, and their birth date. (10 guests in The Parker Annex, 11 in The Parker Home.)

From this modest beginning, the "News" became one of the primary methods of "getting the word out" about the work of Presbyterian Home of Central Pennsylvania. The "News" was printed two or three times each year. Two of the three editions were always printed just prior to Harvest Home Day and Mother's Day— the two most important days on the homes' calendar. The third edition would be published in mid-winter when needed and was sometimes a special edition outlining rules for admission, or marking a significant anniversary in the homes' history.

By 1940 Swaim increased the circulation of the "News" to more than 50,000 copies, with the goal of every member of every constituent church receiving a copy. Swaim put anyone who had any interest in the work of the corporation on the mailing list. He used issues of the "News" in follow-

37

up correspondence with contributors and with other homes for the aging interested in the workings of Presbyterian Home of Central Pennsylvania.

With the 1944 Harvest Home Edition (Vol. IX, No. 1), the "News" took on a new look. From that issue the "News" was published in the popular 8 1/2 by 11-inch "letter-size" format. This format remained the standard for most of the next 40 years with few exceptions. Although four and eight pages were the standard numbers, some editions in the 1950s included as many as 32 pages per issue. The 1950s were, by any measure, the heyday of the "News." Nearly every issue in the 1950s used a full-cover photograph. The pages inside were filled with photos of guests in the several homes. Anniversaries were marked with pages of photos, reprints of speeches, and testimonials by guests. During the fifties, Swaim experimented with colors, with layout sizes and with many other publication details.

During the 1960s, the "News" settled into four- and eight-page issues twice each year. No more 32-page anniversary commemoratives. The second issue of the decade, the 1960 Harvest Home issue, was all cartoons— front to back, eight pages of drawings done by a resident of The Parker Home. Swaim got comments on that issue for years afterwards.

From the beginning, as noted earlier, Bill Swaim did the work of putting together the "News" largely on his own. According to Vivian Cook, a long-time employee of the corporation's central office, one day prior to each publication was set aside strictly for the "News." On that day Swaim would take off his shoes, spread all the material for the latest issue on the floor, and get to work. He left the material only to drop pages for typing on a secretary's desk, then went straight back into the office. At days end, the finished layout was ready. Swaim then put his shoes back on and headed for the printer. (Swaim took his shoes off before beginning work on each issue and worked in white socks.)

For several years in the late 1960s and early 1970s, Martie Kunkle, editor of *The Weekly Bulletin,* Dillsburg, wrote several articles for the "News" and assisted with layout. During these years, News was printed in four and six page editions. At the end of 1972, the "News" suspended publication for three years to centralize all mailings for a very successful capital funds drive held during this period.

In 1975 the "News" resumed publication. For the first two years each issue was loaded with facts about new facilities and sounded somewhat like the issues of the fifties. In 1978 the contents shifted again—this time to lists of contributors and office news. The eighties opened with Lewis Doolittle contributing articles and assisting with layout. For the first four years of this decade, the "News" became a four- to eight-page tabloid with three to four issues each year. His work gave the News a very old-fashioned and homey appearance.

In 1985, the News returned to the eight-page letter-sized format that Bill Swaim favored, following the practices of the days when Swaim took off his shoes and published a very good newsletter. Now that we have the "news" to the present, we should go back to 1938 and catch the important parts of a speech that should have delineated the expansion policy of Presbyterian Home of Central Pennsylvania. It did, but not right away.

Anniversary Celebration at the Parker Home

# 9

# Plans Made, Plans Deferred

*Every man's got to figure to get beat sometime.*
—Joe Louis

In an address given at the tenth anniversary celebration of The Parker Home held October 11, 1938, Bill Swaim gave a speech on the future of the corporation. The speech set the course the trustees had agreed to for the future of the homes. Including, among other things, caring for 100 guests by 1950 and, when possible, opening a "Home-Like Home" in each of the six cooperating presbyteries. That, at least, was the plan, and Swaim liked it. The founders, as we have seen, began working on plans to expand the Parker Farmhouse the day it opened. And again, Mrs. Parker told the trustees that The Parker Annex in Carlisle could be sold at any time with the proceeds benefitting the Farm. Current wisdom said the aging should live out in the country. But Swaim's experience said the opposite.

When Swaim addressed the anniversary gathering he found no dissenters, at least no vocal dissenters. The plan made sense to him. He thought the trustees were also convinced. But bringing 23 tradition-minded people to a new way of thinking could not be accomplished so easily.

The trustees, a conservative group throughout the corporation's history, did not see what Swaim saw. Swaim took the prospective residents to their new homes by himself. The trustees for the most part shared the vision of developing the Parker Farm into a quiet home in the country, the kind of home for the aging that was common at the time and followed the thinking of their time.

Swaim went to the next meeting of the full board in the spring of 1939 with three complete proposals for new sites for homes. One of these sites was Irving College in Mechanicsburg which is still a functioning apartment building today. Swaim's proposals were never heard.

At that meeting on May 23, 1939, in the parlor of The Parker Home, J. Harold Wolf looked out the front window and pointed to a corn field across the road. He said, "We will build the next home there," pointing at the recently seeded field. The assembled trustees assented. The motion was duly seconded and carried. Two years later The Farm Annex (renamed The Manor shortly after its dedication) opened right where J. Harold Wolf said it would.

Besides Swaim, only the treasurer, S. Sharpe Huston, dissented. And Huston expressed that dissent only in private after the meeting. Huston was a quiet man, a banker with a solid reputation for wise investments. Huston told Swaim that a large building out on a farm in Newville would give the corporation no equity. Huston kept his own counsel and, like Swaim, would work hard on the new home.

When the motion carried the planning began. The proposed building would cost $80,000. The treasury held only $20,000 for the project. The additional $60,000 was raised by issuing annuities, and generous giving by supporters of the home over the next four years. The $20,000 debt that remained in 1943 was retired by a new resident who brought more than $20,000 to the treasury.

To this day Swaim calls J. Harold Wolf and William S. Middleton the two board members who, "Made a man out of me." Swaim had an agenda for the expansion of the corporation that he now knew was a radical departure from the thinking of the rest of the board. He also found to his dismay that he had not communicated that vision to anyone on the board with real clarity. Swaim was, by his own account, caught unprepared. But he was not to get caught again.

In the coming years Swaim sent material for the meeting of the full board of trustees in ten to twenty page packages in the weeks and months before each meeting. This practice let Swaim set much of the agenda for the meeting. Swaim's planning reached the level of an art—if trustee's meetings can be so elevated—during the late-1960s when John Killian was president of the board and Swaim was administrator. These meetings would travel quickly from point to point down a forty to fifty item agenda with two to three minutes used for each item. Swaim said with some pride that he could write the minutes of the meeting before the meeting began.

Soon after Swaim took over as full time administrator and for the first years of his tenure he would go to the board meetings with a sharp pain in his neck and upper back. He was nervous and edgy. As he began to prepare more fully for the meetings, the pain went away.

The disappointment Swaim felt leaving the May 1939 meeting of the board are expressed in the lead paragraph of the next issue of "The Newville Home News"—the 1939 Harvest Home edition:

"At the request of the Board of Trustees, the Executive Committee is ready to present to them a tentative plan for the erection of a new annex on the Newville Home farm. After the Board of Trustees had refused, last May, to purchase old properties it was decided to build at Home. The idea took fire, and burst into flame when the Trustees walked across the driveway and found "acres of diamonds," speaking of sites, in the field nearest the Newville Home."

Swaim's enthusiasm for The Manor, as the Newville Home Farm Annex would eventually be called, did not sway his determination to scatter "Small, Home-like Homes" throughout the six presbyteries. The next time the Parker Farm would be developed would be seven years after Swaim's retirement, when the Swaim Health Center opened up the hill from the Parker farmhouse.

After The Farm Annex, every home that Presbyterian Home of Central Pennsylvania built or developed until Swaim's retirement would fit the "Small, Scattered, Home-like Homes for the Aging" pattern he ennunciated in 1938. Swaim, appropriately enough, gave the dedicatory address at the opening of the Swaim Health Center in 1977—the first development of the Parker Farm since 1941.

He was honored to have a Home named for him, but times had changed and the Swaim Health Center was, in many respects, the Home Swaim never would have built. Here was a nursing home (Swaim was against the corporation owning nursing homes during his tenure, for economic reasons that changed drastically in the 1960s) built out on the Parker Farm (which Swaim resisted developing) as part of the first Continuing Care Campus operated by Presbyterian Homes, Inc. The campus concept brings together all levels of care in the same place. Swaim said during his tenure as administrator that nursing homes and residence homes should be "out of sight of one another" The Home that bears the Swaim name is, in short, an accumulation of characteristics that were wrong for his time, but, with all the changes in caring for the aging in the intervening decades are right for the present.

In 1939 The Farm Annex was taking shape. It would soon be the fourth and the largest of the homes. The work of building The Manor would give Swaim the full-time job as administrator of the Homes that he had been after for more than five years. The home Swaim didn't want gave him his career.

The Manor Home

# 10

# The Manor

*All that is not forbidden is permitted.* —Harry W. Keeny, President of the board, Presbyterian Home of Central Pennsylvania

With the opening of The Manor (first called The Farm Annex) double occupancy rooms were gone forever from the residential homes of Presbyterian Home of Central Pennsylvania. Harry Keeny's rule, which is the epigraph of this chapter, came about in response to pleas for lists of rules for guests in the homes. The trustees had a file of "Rules for Inmates" accumulated from various other homes. These lists never left their meetings. The corporate policy of building and buying "Small, Scattered, Home-like Homes for the Aging" without posted rules, without double rooms, and with personal allowances even for those guests who entered the home penniless, added up to a central concern for the dignity and happiness of their guests.

The opening of The Manor extended the corporate philosophy by adding beauty to the list of requisites for a home. At its opening in January of 1941, The Manor was the largest of the homes to date. The two-story structure was built entirely of native limestone from the Morrison Quarry in nearby Plainfield. Its rooms would house 21 guests and the staff to run the home. Each of the guest's rooms was furnished with a desk and chair, a bed, an easy chair, and a dresser—all made from maple.

Common rooms included a sun parlor and a reception room in addition to the dining room. Among the furnishings donated to the new home were a grand piano for the reception room and a 390-pound mahogany sideboard for

45

the dining room. The building itself is T-shaped with single story common rooms forming the cross of the T at either side of the main building. The two-story main residential section of the building stretches straight back from the entrance away from the main driveway.

At the approval of the plans for the building, the trustees had only $20,000 of the needed $80,000 to open the home. The balance was financed through gifts, through annuities, and finally through a resident who entered the home two years after its opening. She had applied saying she could not pay even the admission fee. Bill Swaim went to meet her and told her that her financial position would not affect her application. When the woman was certain the home accepted penniless guests, she began showing Swaim bank books with enough to cover the $20,000 + that remained of the debt for construction of The Manor.

With the debt cleared on The Manor, the trustees would have been free to expand further, but the year the new guest brought in the money that would pay off the debt on The Manor was 1943. American soldiers were fighting on Pacific Islands, in North Africa, and in Italy. All building materials were restricted to use for the war effort so expansion would have to wait—or so it would seem.

Bill Swaim wrote a letter proposing to expand The Parker Annex in Carlisle based on the fact that every room added to the home would free a house, often a large house, occupied only by one elderly widow. Swaim's proposal was eventually accepted by the government on its merits for relieving the universal housing shortage during the war. Other delays conspired to slow the addition, but the project did go forward and in 1948, a seven room addition opened at The Parker Annex in Carlisle raising the total capacity of the building to 18 and the capacity of the four homes to 61.

A court decision in 1945 freed the Parker Estate for use by Presbyterian Home of Central Pennsylvania for the care of the aging. As the 1940s ended, the corporate balance sheet looked better than it ever had. One provision of Mrs. Parker's will restricted $40,000 of the estate for use in the construction of an orphanage which was to be built on the

Parker Farm in the mid-1940s. At the time of Mrs. Parker's death, orphaned children were principally cared for in state or in church institutions. Legislation enacted in the 1930s as part of President Roosevelt's New Deal and other initiatives changed the direction of orphan care from institutions to foster care in private homes.

The new legislation was emptying orphanages around the country. In a brief presented in the Court of Common Pleas, Cumberland County, the trustees, represented by President William S. Middleton and others, argued that changes in the legislation and in the direction of child care in the country worked against Presbyterian Home of Central Pennsylvania erecting an orphanage. He argued that Mrs. Parker could not have anticipated these legislative changes when she wrote her will in 1928. Lewis Parker, as Mrs. Parker's only living relative, wrote a letter supporting the shift of the restricted portion of his mother's estate to the care of the aging.

As a result of the court's decision, the trustees established the Ellen Parker Bureau for Child Care and named Bill Swaim its administrator. In the years that followed, the Ellen Parker Bureau for Child Care handled requests from constituent churches and church members about foster care and adoption of orphaned children.

So the 1940s saw the corporation expand little, but consolidate its position as a provider of housing for the aging. Paying off The Manor and settling the final questions in the Parker will also left the corporation free to pursue its goal of establishing homes for the aging in each of the six constituent presbyteries. In the 1950s the number of homes doubled to eight. These four homes were located in three different presbyteries, including Chester Presbytery, the seventh constituent presbytery of Presbyterian Home of Central Pennsylvania.

The Kennett Square Home

# 11

# New Homes from Old Mansions

*Growth is the only evidence of life.* —John Henry, Cardinal Newman

The 1950s were years of great promise and of promises fulfilled for Presbyterian Home of Central Pennsylvania. The first issue of *The Presbyterian Home News* in 1950 commemorated the tenth anniversary of The Manor. Most of the issues's eight pages were devoted to pictures and information about this largest of the four homes. Tucked underneath the standard masthead on this issue was, for the first time, the logo "Small, Scattered, Home-Like Homes for the Aging." The plans were going ahead for a new home in Hazleton, Lehigh Presbytery, so the plans for moving out of Carlisle Presbytery into the other five constituent presbyteries were finally becoming a reality.

On page seven of the same issue were two small news items about Bill Swaim. The first item, entitled "Swaim Service" recorded Swaim's attendance at the first National Conference on Aging held in Washington, D.C. The same item said Swaim spoke at a Lutheran Welfare Conference. His subject—"Small, Scattered, Home-like Homes for the Aging."

The second item recorded a visit to the homes by the Executive Secretary of a home for the aging in Illinois. According to the item, the official was so impressed by the "Home-Like Homes" plan that he returned to Illinois to persuade his governing board that their own organization should adopt this plan.

On March 13, 1951, the corporation bought the Pardee

49

Mansion, 126 North Church Street, Hazleton, for $45,000. Renovations began two days later to make the home ready for 18 guests. The building was built by the Pardee family of Hazleton in 1924 at a cost of more than $200,000. Its 23-inch thick stone walls encased a steel frame and supported a tile roof. All of the windows in the sun parlor, and some other windows were made from leaded glass.

On August 20 the first guest arrived. The dedication service was held October 18. The Hazleton Home raised the total capacity of the five homes to 78, but, according to Bill Swaim, this home and its companion home, The Hazleton Cottage which opened in 1952, actually did little to relieve the problem of long waiting lists. Building a home in Lehigh Presbytery quickly increased the number of local applicants. Of the first sixteen guests, five transferred from homes in Newville and Carlisle to be nearer their home towns. Ten of the eleven remaining guests were from Lehigh, Lackawanna, and Northumberland Presbyteries from towns less than fifty miles away. (The eleventh guest in this group was from Clarion Presbytery in the west.)

A year later, October 23, 1952, was dedication day for the Hazleton Cottage, the sixth home. The Hazleton Cottage was actually the garage of the Pardee Mansion. It was renovated and converted to housing for eight guests. The garage was built with the same stone and boasted the same thick walls as the mansion itself. One particular advantage of The Hazleton Cottage was its entrance. The garage door was simply walled over for the front entrance which meant no steps for entrance and exit. Just three steps on a small porch can become a significant barrier for people in their 70s and 80s. Entrance and exit at the cottage was on a level drive rather than the several steps in front of The Hazleton Home.

Seven of the first eight guests admitted to The Hazleton Cottage came to the home from nearby towns in Lehigh and Lackawanna Presbyteries. The eighth guest came from Carlisle Presbytery. Her home was in Hershey, so Hazleton was not much further from her home than Carlisle.

Despite increased applications coming to the office from the northern presbyteries, the next expansion moved southeast. In June 1951, Bill Swaim spoke at a meeting of Chester Presbytery officials. At the end of his talk about Presbyterian Home of Central Pennsylvania a man at the back of the hall asked if their presbytery could join the corporation. Swaim said he would ask the trustees. He did and the negotiations began.

Several formulas were proposed and rejected. One called for a $50,000 admission fee to bring the Chester Presbytery in as a full member of the corporation. The formula finally agreed upon opened the seventh home in 1954. Chester Presbytery, for its admission to the corporation, agreed to purchase and furnish a home for the aging within the presbytery.

The home they opened was the former Scarlett Mansion on Lincoln Street in Kennett Square. It was renovated to provide accommodations for 20 guests. The first floor of the mansion was used for common rooms, the second and third floors provided rooms for 20 guests and for the matron. Swaim spoke at an open house inspection held on May 2, 1954, twenty-one years after he was first elected a trustee of the corporation. Eleven months later the first guests moved into the new home.

The additional capacity the new home brought to the corporation did little to relieve the waiting list. Of the first 21 guests (one woman died only two months after she was admitted) four transferred from other homes in Newville, two came to the home from Lehigh Presbytery, and the other 15 all came from Chester Presbytery. With total capacity now at 104, waiting lists remained the rule.

The following year, in 1956, plans got underway for the fourth home to open in the 1950s. Unlike the other three homes, which were purchased, The Mount Joy Home, (later The Schock Home) came to the corporation as a bequest along with an endowment fund given by Mr. and Mrs. Clarence Schock of Mount Joy. The mansion, located at 37 West Main Street, like the other homes acquired in the 1950s, is old and substantial. It was built in 1879 with 18-inch thick brick walls. As part of the bequest, Clarence Schock bought adjoining property to allow for expansion of the home.

According to Bill Swaim, the bequest and property came to the home because a friend and neighbor of Mr. and Mrs. Schock, Miss Ida Leib, entered The Parker Home several years before and loved it. The Schock's visited the home and through discussions with Miss Leib, decided to leave their home and part of their estate to Presbyterian Home of Central Pennsylvania.

The main house provided four bedrooms for guests on the second floor, five on the third floor, with the first floor used for common areas. A new wing that connected the garage at the back of the house added thirteen bedrooms, and the large garage was converted to an infirmary for a total of 22 rooms for guests plus accommodations for the staff.

The home opened in 1958 bringing total accommodations to 130 rooms in eight homes in four different presbyteries. The Mount Joy Home cleared the waiting list in Donegal Presbytery as soon as it opened. Like the other homes opening in new presbyteries, this home soon created a waiting list all its own for those wanting to live near home. The total waiting list climbed to 90 the following year.

The year 1959 closed a successful decade for Presbyterian Home of Central Pennsylvania. With new homes going up at the rate of one every two years and the waiting list growing, more expansion was needed, and expansion plans were underway. With the realignment of presbyteries accomplished in 1959, the number of constituent Presbyteries was back to six (Chester Presbytery was now part of Donegal Presbytery) but the realigned borders actually added more than seventy churches to the constituent area. Clarion Presbytery was incorporated in a new presbytery named Kiskiminetas. Plans were underway the same year to open a home in Kittanning, part of the expanded area in the western part of Pennsylvania that included the former Clarion Presbytery.

Other changes presented problems. Since the 1940s, Bill Swaim had been urging the trustees to amend the charter to remove the restrictive language in article two—that the corporation could only care for "White Presbyterians." In 1953 Swaim began to travel throughout the several presbyteries urging them to support the change. Though the Federal government had not yet passed the comprehensive civil rights legislation, Swaim could see it coming, and see the threat it posed to the corporation. On a personal level Swaim had been embarrassed to admit that the corporation he administered had such language in its charter. The change, of course, did come—two years ahead of any legislation that would have forced it. In 1962 the charter was completely revised with all the restrictive language removed.

Another change many of the trustees sought since 1951 was in the office. They felt Swaim should have an assistant. Swaim felt otherwise, but in his case, the change came after the problem occurred. In 1963 the man who had spent his life caring for other aging people found he wasn't immune to the problems of aging himself.

Construction of the Williamsport Presbyterian Home

# 12

# New Homes from the Ground Up

*The great use of life is to spend it for something that outlasts life.* —William James

The first two years of the 1960s saw Bill Swaim and the corporation riding high. Eight homes were open, double the number open just ten years before, three more homes were on the drawing board (in each of the three presbyteries still without homes), and six of the eight existing homes were expanding. The 130 rooms available would nearly double to 222 rooms when all the projects were completed. In 1960, corporate policy changed to allow admission of men to the homes for the first time, although the first male guest did not move in until 1963.

All of the goals the trustees had set in earlier years would be exceeded by the projects on the drawing board, and who could tell what the rest of the decade would bring. Swaim was still administering the growing corporation with a staff of two and by any estimation, doing fine. The first issue of The Presbyterian Homes News in this decade, the 1960 Mother's Day edition, showed a front cover photo of a sign being nailed up at the site of The Kittanning Home, the first home built by the corporation since The Manor opened in 1941. Inside was a list of the current and proposed projects. But a more important issue followed six months later. Inside the 1960 Harvest Home issue of *The Presbyterian Homes News* were five and one-half pages of cartoons by Miss Laura Hinckley, a resident of The Parker Home. That Swaim could devote an issue to cartoons with a half-dozen partially-funded expansion projects pending bespoke limit-less confidence.

An expansion fund campaign got underway the following year with Mrs. Mamie Doud Eisenhower of First United Presbyterian Church of Gettysburg acting as Honorary Campaign Chairman. By 1965 the expansion fund had raised a half-million dollars against a goal of $800,000. The shortfall could be expected, even the shortfall of collecting only $518,000 of $693,000 pledged, but with all the expansion going forward the accounting was tight. John D. Killian, president of the board of trustees during the latter half of the 1960s, remembers those days as a time when the books were sometimes balanced with bequests from persons not yet dead. Albert Schartner, the assistant administrator of the corporation from 1964 through 1970, remembers paydays going by when he and Swaim paid the office help with the funds available and waited for the mail to see if the money would come in so they themselves would be paid. The money always came in and the corporation grew. In fact they expanded further than the projections at the opening of the decade.

Of the projects listed earlier, two of the three new homes—one in Kittanning, and one in Williamsport—opened in 1964 and 1966, respectively. The Scranton residential Home never materialized. However, Geneva House, which opened in Scranton in 1972, is an apartment complex for the aging built by Presbyterian Homes of Central Pennsylvania as a subsidiary corporation. It brought the corporation into each of the constituent presbyteries. The expansion of the homes in Hazleton, The Kennett Square Home, The Carlisle Home, The Parker Home, and The Newville Home all went ahead as planned and added two to six rooms to each of these facilities.

In addition, the corporation expanded by backing an independent apartment complex in Harrisburg known as Presbyterian Apartments, Inc. Plans for the 23-story complex date back to the beginning of the decade. The building finally opened in 1967 with 165 apartments for the elderly. In the same year, the Ware Apartments opened in Oxford. The Ware Apartments were seven apartments in a remodeled mansion donated by State Senator (and later Congressman) John H. Ware, III. More than 13 acres of land just a few blocks from the center of Oxford were given to the homes along with the mansion. Ten years later this land would be developed into one of the largest of the Presbyterian homes.

In 1961 Bill Swaim celebrated his 55th birthday. That year also marked ten years since the trustees first suggested Swaim needed an assistant. Swaim was still three years away from adding an assistant and he was the picture of health, indeed, he was well-known throughout the various homes for his health and vigor. He would, on visiting some of the homes, jump over the sofa in the parlor without touching it. Back in the office he would jump over the shoulders of his secretary while she was standing up when he felt particularly good. But it wasn't his legs that gave him trouble.

In 1963 while Bill Swaim was driving to a weekend speaking engagement in another state, he started seeing "little fish" swimming in his right eye. He stopped for lunch at a Rotary hall on the way and talked to a doctor who assured him that he was only experiencing "floaters" and that it was nothing to be concerned about. When he got to the hotel, Swaim became more concerned and called an eye specialist he knew back home. The doctor was alarmed. He told Swaim to be very careful and get home as soon as possible. The problem was not floaters but a nearly completely detached retina. The doctor operated and restored Swaim's sight, but Swaim was not back to full-time work for nearly six weeks. Now the search for an assistant became serious.

Swaim interviewed two men he knew for the job and "made the mistake" of telling them the breadth of his work. Upon hearing about Swaim's schedule, neither pursued the job further. Albert L. Schartner, a very successful Presbyterian pastor in the western part of Pennsylvania, was mentioned to Swaim by a mutual acquaintance. Schartner, who was 32 years old at the time, had increased the size of his congregation ten-fold in just seven years in the church he pastored in Irwin, Pennsylvania. Schartner took over a church recently split over doctrine and built it up to a higher level than it had ever been. The young minister had offers of much larger pastorates from two other congregations, but his real interest was work with the aging.

On a day that Swaim called the most successful day of his life, May 3, 1964, he went to Irwin to hear Schartner preach, then had dinner with the Schartner family after the service. On the following Tuesday, Swaim recommended Schartner to the board of trustees. The next month Schartner attended Swaim's short course for administrators for that year, and on July 1, he started work as Assistant Administrator of Presbyterian Homes of Central Pennsylvania.

The following year would see Swaim agree to surgery on his hands. The surgery left him unable to type and do other office tasks without chronic pain. Despite the surgery in the 1960s, Swaim accomplished the three things he was most proud of in his long career with the corporation.

The first was The Williamsport Home. This home was the last built solely as a residential home by the corporation. According to Swaim, this home represents his most mature thinking and was the only home in which he "really had his say." The home is a stone building just a few blocks from the center of town on a tree-lined street. Like The Kittanning Home, it houses 24 guests and was built from the ground up by the corporation. It follows every legislative guideline on exits and hallways and the several other problems that would force the closure of the older mansions in the years that followed. Swaim credits the quality of this home's construction, from its slate roof to its copper drains, with helping to convince the corporation's largest benefactor, Dr. N. B. Steward, that he would be leaving his life's earnings to an institution that would use them wisely. Swaim was so proud of this home that he saved all the relevant documents in two, 3- inch thick binders that are in the corporation's files.

Second on Swaim's list of achievements was Presbyterian Apartments, Inc., in Harrisburg. Although this 23-story tower with its 165 apartments is a separate corporation, Swaim served as developer for the project.

Located just three blocks from the center of Harrisburg, the apartment complex houses about 200 residents in 124 studio apartments and 41 one-bedroom units. The Housing and Urban Development Administration (HUD) loaned the money for the building and subsidizes the rent of needy residents. Rent for all residents is based on a percentage of their income.

Swaim's personal enthusiasm for the project (it's the place he chose to live when he retired) is based on the construction. Every support system—plumbing, ventilation, electric lines, fire control lines—is completely accessible and repairable through the walls and the roof. Swaim is sure the building can last 500 years.

Third on Swaim's list was the success of Mrs. Thelma Winters of Wheeling, West Virginia. Mrs. Winters attended Swaim's short course for administrators in 1965. That he was impressed with her was evident in her assignment— she was named supervisor of the new Williamsport Home which Swaim considered the best home. Swaim said he learned much from her common sense in dealing with people. While Mrs. Winters was proving herself a most able and charming supervisor in Williamsport, Swaim's work for the corporation was drawing to a close. An office building in Dillsburg opened in 1967 along with Presbyterian Apartments, Inc., in Harrisburg. These were the last buildings opened while Swaim served as administrator.

The first task Swaim assigned to his new assistant, Albert Schartner, was case work. Soon after, the work was divided between "inside," which Schartner handled and "outside," which was Swaim's province. Schartner handled the case work, administered the office, served as secretary to the board and to the executive committee, and studied the administration of nursing homes. Swaim did the public relations work—including, as ever, *The Presbyterian Homes News*—spoke at churches and civic groups, represented the corporation at all official functions, and headed all the construction projects.

By 1969, the chronic pain from Swaim's surgery, and the confidence he placed in Schartner, helped him to decide it was time to retire. Under Swaim's administration the corporation had grown from a small farmhouse in Newville housing eleven women to a corporation with a national reputation housing nearly 200 aging people in nine homes (The Andrews Home closed in 1968) and a small apartment house, as well as 200 more in an apartment complex in Harrisburg.

This last year of the 1960s marked a change for the country as well as for the corporation. Americans were living longer than ever and modern medical technology was extending the time older Americans could live at home. The need for nursing care for these older persons was fast increasing, at the same time the need for residential care was declining. In 1969, work began to convert part of The Schock Home in Mount Joy into the first nursing home operated by Presbyterian Homes of Central Pennsylvania. The corporation had grown for 42 years on the narrow track of providing "Small, Scattered, Home-Like Homes for the Aging." Beginning in 1970 growth would be coupled with expansion into new areas of service for the aging—nursing homes, apartments, independent living units, and home health care—and the residential homes, like all good soldiers, would begin to fade away.

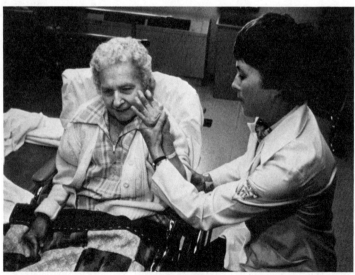

Nursing Care

# 13

# Plans for a New Decade

*The growth of a large business is merely the survival of the fittest. . .The American Beauty rose can be produced in the splendor and fragrance which bring cheer to its beholder only by sacrificing the early buds which grow up around it.*
—John Kenneth Galbraith

The February 1970 meeting of the executive committee board of trustees opened like any other with the accepting of the minutes of the previous meeting and all the routine parlimentary proceedings that such meetings generate. After more than an hour of preliminaries, the new administrator of the corporation, Albert Schartner made a presentation that would become the plan of business for Presbyterian Homes of Central Pennsylvania for the next 13 years—the point at which all the goals were reached or were incorporated into a new strategic plan for the rest of the century that was adopted by the board that year.

Like Bill Swaim's plan for putting "Small, Scattered, Home-like Homes for the Aging" in every presbytery—the speech was short, and the implementation was gradual, but Schartner's "Strategy for the Presbyterian Homes" would change the corporation fundamentally.

The printed summary of the presentation is divided into four parts. The first, entitled "The Value of Homelike Homes," briefly describes the advantages of the only type of home the corporation operated at that time—the residential care home. It says:

"Because homelike, residential Homes having 15 or 20 people provide a most desirable style of life for the fortunate few selected to guestship, the residents benefit greatly from the security, excellent diet and care, companionship, and the personal attention they enjoy in the family atmosphere."

But the next section, entitled "The Peril of Home-like Homes," listed seven current reasons why this type of care should not dominate the work of the corporation in the future. Economic, medical, societal, and political reasons are cited to support Schartner's contention that residential boarding care should be de-emphasized in favor of other types of care. But the strongest reason for the shift to nursing care and independent living is part of the list of advantages of Home-like Homes. It's "the fortunate few" who can live in this type of facility.

If the corporation were going to expand, it must, according to Schartner, broaden its ministry. "The Residential Homes are designed to house well, able, active, ambulatory, older persons" is the phrase that opens the "Perils" section of the presentation. The corporation housed fewer people in the nine residential homes then operating than lived in Presbyterian Apartments, Inc., in Harrisburg.

Schartner's nine-point plan to meet changing needs of the elderly was less revolutionary in its execution than in its wording. First, the proposed nursing care facilities would be built and acquired near the present residential care facilities, with a preference for the residential homes that were most likely to remain open in the decades to follow.

Because the nursing homes could operate in the black after startup costs were absorbed, the nursing homes offered the most hope of perpetuating residential care as a part of the corporation's work. Nursing care patients receive reimbursement for their care from Medicare and from Medicaid. The money earned from nursing care could help to subsidize residential care guests who receive no income beyond Social Security payments and so cannot afford the high actual costs of residential care (more than $30 per day in 1985).

The plan, as presented in 1970, put the corporation on a path that would triple its total capacity within 15 years and possibly double that figure in the 15 years that follow. In fact, by 1980 all of the goals that Schartner set forth were either accomplished or underway. When compared to

Swaim's plan in 1938, Schartner's was more ambitious, but Schartner started his work from a more solid footing. By 1970, the duties and responsibilities of the executive were clear. The trustees also worked from many years of progress in good economic conditions. Swaim started in the last years of the depression with an influential and traditionally-minded trustee waiting to trip the young administrator at the first turn.

In 1970, the first nursing home operated by Presbyterian Homes, Inc., opened in The Schock Home in Mount Joy. This small nursing facility (less than 20 patients) served as a testing ground for the policies and procedures the corporation would use in the larger homes acquired in the coming years. The first administrator of that home was Stephen Proctor, who still holds the title of the youngest administrator of any Presbyterian Homes, Inc., facility. He was 20-years-old when Schartner hired him.

Schartner°s life has seen seven-year cycles. He spent nearly seven years in college and in seminary. His first pastorate lasted seven years. The next seven years began July 1, 1964, reading files in the rear of the one-room main office of Presbyterian Homes of Central Pennsylvania and ended in 1971 with Schartner serving his first year as administrator of the corporation. In the next year, the first nursing home was opened in Mount Joy and negotiations were nearly completed for buying Forest Park Health Center in Carlisle. Geneva House, the first project developed by the corporation in Lackawanna Presbytery, was nearing completion after several delays. The next seven years would see five nursing homes open, three residential homes close, and the total capacity of the facilities tripled.

Ground breaking for Geneva House in Scranton, Pa.

# 14

# Openings, Closings, and Rapid Growth

*Progress is what happens when impossibility yields to necessity.* — Arnold Glasow

Wednesday, August 18, 1971, saw the ground-breaking ceremony for the first project developed by Presbyterian Homes of Central Pennsylvania in the 1970s. Known as Geneva House, Inc., this nine-story complex included 105 one-bedroom and efficiency apartments. Like Presbyterian Apartments, Inc., in Harrisburg, the complex was built with a loan from the federal Housing and Urban Development Administration.

The apartment complex began with a charter in 1968 incorporating Geneva House as an independent corporation. Bill Swaim initiated the project after two separate attempts to open residential care homes in Scranton were dropped. Schartner continued the work after Swaim's retirement and the building opened less than a year after the ground-breaking ceremony. Presbyterian Homes of Central Pennsylvania now provided housing for the elderly in all six of the cooperating presbyteries that together formed the corporation nearly forty years after the first home opened in 1928.

With facilities in all six presbyteries, development plans came back to Carlisle Presbytery where the first four Presbyterian Homes were opened. On August 1, 1972, the corporation bought a 3-year-old, 96-bed nursing home in Carlisle operated by a proprietary corporation called Forest Park Nursing Homes, Inc. It was renamed Forest Park

Health Center and became the tenth unit of Presbyterian Homes of Central Pennsylvania. It was also the first Presbyterian Home designed exclusively as a nursing home. Two years earlier, The Schock Home in Mount Joy had been partially converted from service as a residential home to a nursing home, but it would be returned to strictly residential service in 1974.

Even before the purchase papers for Forest Park Health Center were signed, negotiations were underway to buy the 76-bed Sycamore Manor nursing home in Mountoursville. Located less than four miles from The Williamsport Home, buying this facility followed Schartner's strategic plan of buying or building nursing homes close to the existing residential homes. Proximity meant that persons living in residential homes that needed nursing care could get that care without travelling far from familiar surroundings. Developing near existing sites made use of the goodwill that the residential homes had developed over the years to assure community support.

Sycamore Manor Health Center, as it was named, was developed in the 1960s as a proprietary home. Plans for expanding the home were drawn soon after the facility opened and completed less than two years later. With expansion to 123 beds, Sycamore Manor Health Center became the largest nursing care facility in the corporation and is still the largest in 1985. An interim loan gave the corporation ownership of the facility late in 1972.

The following year saw the purchase of a third nursing home, Central Park Nursing Home in Allentown. Like Forest Park Health Center, the Allentown facility was built in the 1960s as a for- profit home. At its opening it was renamed Lehigh Manor and remodeled. The renovations made this three-story brick building a combined nursing home and residential home with 98 nursing care beds and ten residential care rooms. The reason the property could be purchased so soon after the purchase of Forest Park Health Center was a bequest of more than $230,000 by Ellen Lewis. With the opening of Lehigh Manor, the nursing care capacity of the corporation now exceeded the number of residential care rooms—just three years after the first nursing care facility opened in Mount Joy.

With three new nursing homes opened in as many years, 1975 opened with consolidation in the office and bigger plans underway for the future. One reason that the expansion could go forward so quickly was a very successful capital funds drive in 1973 and 1974 that raised much of the money needed to expand. Mrs. Mamie Doud Eisenhower of First Presbyterian Church in Gettysburg again served as honorary chairman of the campaign as she had in the fund raising campaign held 12 years before. The Honorable Senator John Ware, III, was honorary co-chairman of the campaign, with trustee Howard Hunsworth serving as the chairman of the campaign. It was in 1974 that plans were made to build a nursing home on the Parker Farm, the first development of that property since The Manor opened in 1941. Plans got underway in 1975 for Oxford Manor-The Steward Home, a combined nursing and residential care facility to be built on the Ware property in Oxford.

In 1975, after a three-year suspension, The Presbyterian Homes News was published again. Publication had been halted in 1972 because of the capital funds drive mentioned above. Semi-annual mailings with short announcements were distributed during that period, but all the mailings during the fund drive were coordinated to that effort. That first issue announced the latest change in the corporate name and the rationale behind it. Presbyterian Homes of Central Pennsylvania became Presbyterian Homes, Inc. Central Pennsylvania had been a misnomer from the beginning, considering the location of the presbyteries the corporation represented. By 1975, with homes open from Allentown to Kittanning—more than 3/4ths of the length of Pennsylvania— "Central Pennsylvania" described the corporation even less well.

Stephen Proctor, administrator of The Schock Home, was granted leave from his duties to attend North Texas State University in 1975 to begin work on a master of health care administration degree. He attended classes with John Earwood, a former combat helicopter pilot, who came to Presbyterian Homes, Inc., as their first graduate intern in health care administration. Earwood and Proctor completed their course work together. Proctor's internship was waived because of his experience; Earwood came to Pennsylvania expecting the sort of "busy work" often given to interns.

Soon after he arrived Earwood began work developing a financial procedures manual that was put into use, not into an "internship projects" file. At the completion of his internship, Earwood was hired as the administrator-elect of the Swaim Health Center in Newville. Proctor became administrator-elect of the Oxford facility after his return from graduate school.

Training had been part of the corporate program long before Earwood arrived. From 1957 to 1970, Bill Swaim taught annual courses in the administration of homes for the aging in Dillsburg. Called "Short Courses," they allowed Swaim to share his long years of experience with people from around the country at a time when few colleges offered courses designed for the administrators of long-term care facilities. Albert Schartner attended the Short Course in 1964 just before he began his work as assistant administrator of the Homes.

As administrators-elect, Earwood and Proctor worked with construction crews, trained and hired a new staff, and had freedom and responsibility that were "nothing like the Army," in Earwood's words. Soon after the Swaim Health Center opened, Earwood established an internship program at the home for nursing students at nearby Shippensburg College, then established an internship program for aides from Big Spring Area High School. He cites the practical benefits of such an arrangement, but the human benefits exceed the practical. Nurses, and especially aides, trained under this arrangement work more confidently from the first day they work alone. Proctor established in-service training programs at his facility which he now oversees in all the nursing facilities of Presbyterian Homes, Inc. These in-service courses keep employees at every level aware of all the latest procedures and programs that affect their specific work. For the residents, this means better care. And residents who know the staff is trained and confident are happier for that knowledge.

The year 1977 marked three significant events that would set up a further expansion of the corporation in the years that followed. Two new homes opened that year. Both facilities were primarily nursing homes and both were the first nursing homes built by the corporation from the ground up. More important for the future, both were built on large tracts of ground with room for development.

In the spring of 1977 Oxford Manor-The Steward Home, opened on an 18-acre tract of land just outside the town of Oxford. The site was donated almost twelve years before by John H. Ware, III, along with a mansion that had been converted to apartments for the aging in 1967. This facility included a 100-bed skilled and intermediate nursing care facility and a 40-room residential care wing with, among other amenities, private bath facilities for each resident. With 140 persons in the same building, Oxford Manor became the largest single facility under the management of Presbyterian Homes, Inc.

A few months later the Swaim Health Center, a 48-bed, nursing home, opened in Newville on the Parker Farm, just up the hill from the first of the homes—The Parker Home. The new home was dedicated on June 12, 1977, with Swaim himself delivering the keynote speech. Early in the speech he told the audience how well-chosen he thought this site for a home that bears his name:

"Newville is an appropriate locale for a visible reminder of my name. My only installed pastorate was here (1933-1940). In this town our two daughters spent their first years. The family owns a burial plot in the Big Spring Presbyterian Cemetery. We loved the people and the community life; but, with a young minister and the worst years of the economic depression, the pastorate was uneventful. The loudest I ever heard the doxology sung was on the Sunday I resigned."

His speech continued in this good-humored tone to recount the years of his administration of the corporation.

For the direction the corporation would take in the following years, opening these two homes marked not only expansion, but a rationalization of the care the Homes would provide. These two nursing homes were built on spacious grounds that would be the basis of Continuing Care Campuses—facilities on which every level of care from independent living to skilled nursing care is available on the same grounds. The Swaim Health Center and The Manor on the Parker Farm provided nursing care and residential care on the same property. Oxford Manor-The Steward Home provided nursing care and residential care in the same building. The addition of independent living to form a Continuing Care Campus would begin the following year.

Opening these two homes were the first two of the three significant events of 1977. The third was the reorganization of the board of trustees. Howard Hunsworth ended a four year term as president of the board that year. His successor, the Rev. Russell Weer, was the first chairman of the board of trustees. The reorganization of the board made the executive vice president of the corporation (formerly the administrator) the president and chief executive officer.

In 1971, Albert Schartner's title was changed from administrator of the corporation to executive vice president when the supervisors of the individual homes were changed to administrators. The increased responsibilities that came to the people who managed the homes made the title administrator more descriptive of their duties. Executive vice president also better described the relationship of the corporate administrator with the administrators of the various facilities.

With the change in titles in 1977, the board defined the executive responsibility of the corporation. The result of that definition and the scope of the responsibility resulted in the title change to President and Chief Executive Officer. Like the corporate name change two years before, the evolution of titles more exactly described the work performed.

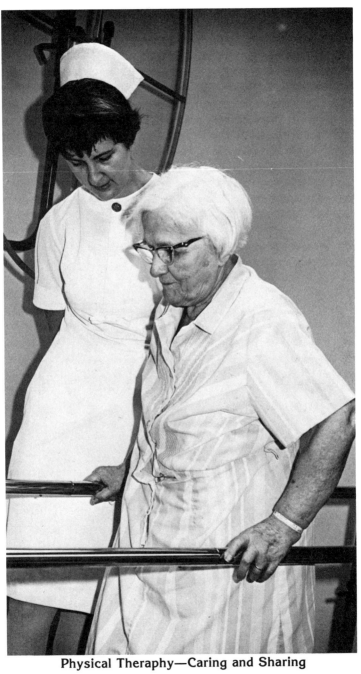

Physical Theraphy—Caring and Sharing

A continuing care campus — Green Ridge Village

# 15

# The Continuing Care Campus

*The art of progress is to preserve order amid change and preserve change amid order.* —Alfred North Whitehead

The year 1978 was the golden anniversary of Presbyterian Homes, Inc. Fifty years earlier nine women moved into the small farmhouse given to the corporation by Mrs. Ellen Ard Parker. In this same year the first apartments opened on the Parker property. The old Parker farm was renamed on its fiftieth anniversary. It was now Green Ridge Village, the first Continuing Care Campus operated by the corporation. In the years that followed the apartment building would add a wing and duplex houses would spring up on lanes built around Swaim Health Center, the central building on the Green Ridge Village campus.

The continuing care campus is a complex set of buildings developed around the simple premise that residents of any community generally would prefer not to move. Continuing Care Campuses offer their residents every level of care for the aging from independent living in apartments or semi-detached houses, through residential care, to both intermediate and skilled nursing care. Residents joining these communities need not leave their homes if they need nursing care—an especially important consideration for older couples, since one person may need nursing care while the other can continue to live independently. The couple needn't be separated for any reason other than hospitalization.

Since the shift between the different levels of care is

based on the needs of the individual, a person who needs skilled nursing care for a period of time could return to residential care or to independent living at any time he or she is able to return. The corporation has a policy dating back to its beginning of holding rooms open for guests who needed nursing care or who were hospitalized. This policy continues for residents of the continuing care campus with the added advantage of having nursing care at home.

After Green Ridge Village became the first continuing care campus, planning began for converting other facilities to this form of operation. By 1984, three facilities would be operating as continuing care campuses with the fourth scheduled to open in the fall of the following year. One of these continuing care campuses was purchased as a nursing home in 1978.

Hutchinson House, The Eliza Cathcart Home, became the sixth nursing home under Presbyterian Homes, Inc., management in 1978. This facility was a convalescent home opened in 1893 in Devon as part of the Stroud Estate. It was reorganized to provide nursing services when it was purchased. Beginning in 1980, this home was converted to a continuing care campus. The new construction saw several delays, but a nursing wing with apartments on its lower level was opened early in 1984. As soon as the nursing patients were transferred from the 90-year-old Hutchinson House to the new nursing wing, renovations began on the old stone mansion. By the fall of 1984 Hutchinson House became a spacious 32-unit residential care facility making this the third continuing care campus operated by Presbyterian Homes, Inc.

The second continuing care campus opened in 1983. In that year, a 42-apartment building attached by a common hall opened at Lehigh Manor, the nursing and residential care facility purchased by the corporation ten years before. In 1983, Lehigh Manor with its new apartment wing had been renamed Westminster Village. Expansion within the main building added four beds to the nursing care capacity bringing the total capacity of this facility to 102 nursing care beds, 10 residential rooms, and 42 independent living apartments.

With residential care, nursing care, independent living, and the continuing care campus now a part of the corporation's work for the elderly, another form of care was added. In the summer of 1983 Community Home-Care Services was created under the direction of the trustees committee on Program, Education, and Special Services. Trustee Michael Busch was largely responsible for bringing this program into being along with June Hoffman, R.N., who became the director of the program. The first Community Home-Care Services office opened in March, 1984 in the Williamsport Presbyterian Home.

Architect's Drawing of the Indiana Presbyterian Home

# 16

# Current and Future Projects

*And in today already walks tomorrow.* —Samuel Taylor Coleridge

The new decade began with the construction of a seventh nursing home. In 1980 Julia Wilson Pound donated a 7-acre tract of land in Indiana, Pennsylvania, that had been part of a dairy farm she and her late husband operated. Plans for construction followed quickly after the donation of the land, and in 1983 Indiana Presbyterian Home opened, a 120-bed nursing care facility. The new home is located less than 30 miles from Kittanning Presbyterian Home and so carries through the 1970 strategic plan of building and buying nursing homes in close proximity to existing residential care homes.

With the opening of Indiana Presbyterian Home, each of the existing residential care homes was now less than 30 miles from a nursing home owned by the corporation. Plans exist to develop the land around Indiana Presbyterian Home with apartments for the aging that will eventually add this home to the list of continuing care campuses.

In the fall of 1984, the central offices in Dillsburg moved to a larger building located at 1217 Slate Hill Road in Camp Hill. In Dillsburg, the administrative offices were in two separate buildings. The Camp Hill building, purchased from the 3M Company, brought all the offices together in one building, making a much smoother operation.

With all the central administrative offices under one roof, and with the goals of the 1970 strategic plan met and in many cases exceeded, 1985 opened with the corporation ready to expand even further. This year saw the first Presbyterian Homes, Inc., facility located outside Pennsylvania open. The groundwork for this new expansion, though, goes back to 1983.

In that year, the trustees' committee for strategy and development, chaired by former board president Howard Hunsworth, presented a strategic plan for the rest of the century. That plan recommended expansion to meet new areas of need and to achieve greater economies of scale into the states that border Pennsylvania on the south and the west with detailed studies of the best areas to consider for expansion.

That same year, Upper Ohio Valley Presbytery, which includes northern West Virginia and a portion of southeastern Ohio, became the seventh cooperating presbytery in Presbyterian Homes, Inc., and the first presbytery to join the corporation from outside the state of Pennsylvania.

Soon after Upper Ohio Valley Presbytery joined the corporation, Mark H. Kennedy of St. Clairsville, Ohio, donated a wooded tract of ground as the site for a retirement community. Construction at Mark H. Kennedy Park began soon after ground-breaking ceremonies in April of 1985.

In 1984 negotiations were completed for the purchase of Courtland Manor, a proprietary nursing home located on a 17-acre tract of ground located just outside of Dover, Delaware, near Delaware State College. When this facility opens under Presbyterian Homes, Inc. management in late 1986, it will be the first nursing home operated by the corporation outside of Pennsylvania.

The first unit of Presbyterian Homes, Inc. to open outside the state of Pennsylvania is a part of its newest form of care for the aging. In the summer of 1985, the Wheeling, West Virginia agency of Community Home-Care Services began serving the community.

With facilities opened and scheduled to open in three neighboring states, growth and expansion are still the words for the future after 57 years caring for the aging. Construction of cottages underway at Oxford Manor—The Steward Home will make that facility the fourth continuing care campus operated by Presbyterian Homes, Inc. One West Penn opened in Carlisle in December of 1984. This 130-apartment complex became the third HUD-sponsored apartment development for the aging managed by the corporation.

The men and women who worked so hard to open and to run a small home for nine "aging ladies" on the Parker Farm almost 60 years ago would find the small work they began had grown beyond their dreams. The Parker Farm alone, now Green Ridge Village, houses more aging residents than the first eight homes put together. But growth and expansion don't tell the whole story. Despite central computers doing accounting that was once done in a ten cent ledger book, and activities budgets at large facilities that exceed the annual budget 50 years ago, the Homes are not so large a corporation that the dignity of their residents gets pushed under a pile of corporate balance sheets.

The corporation president still answers mail from individual residents. Senior staff people visit all the facilities regularly. A kitchen worker at Cathcart home turned down a supervisory job with a pay increase at another home. "They treat me better here and they treat the people that live here better. I'm going to stay here."

A new resident at the Williamsport Home sent the following note to the admissions secretary soon after she entered that home in the spring of 1985:

"Just a note to express my gratitude for the lovely home situation I have been in for a month now. I do thank the Lord for leading me here and for your kind, warm reception. I do feel at home and the residents are so cordial. So many came from this area and have given me, as formerly from this area, a homecoming welcome. Thank you so much."

Satisfied employees and satisfied residents say more about Presbyterian Homes, Inc., than ten history books. The growth that has been the hallmark of the Homes' past is built on this good will. Their future will be built on the same foundation.

# The History of Presbyterian Homes, Inc. Important Dates

This list includes the election of each president and chairman of the board of trustees as well as the election of each president of the women's auxiliary.

1921 — J. Harold Wolf forms the first committee to investigate Presbyterian orphanage.

1923 — Pennsylvania Synod turns down committee's request for orphanage funding. Suggests contiguous presbyteries cooperate to form benevolent work.

1925 — Mrs. Parker gives the Parker Farm in Newville to Presbyterian Home for the Aging incorporated that year in Carlisle.

— Presbyterian Home for the Aging dissolved by founders in favor of cooperative work by seven presbyteries — Carlisle, Northumberland, Lackawanna, Lehigh, Westminster, Clarion, and Huntingdon.

— Huntingdon Presbytery drops out when they are given a partially endowed home for their own presbytery.

1927 — Clarion Presbytery drops out of corporation.

— Presbyterian Home of Central Pennsylvania chartered in Court of Common Pleas, Cumberland County.

— Renovations begin on Parker Farmhouse.

— The Rev. Glenn M. Shaffer named first president of the board of trustees.

1928 — First nine guests move into The Parker Home, Newville.

1929 — Women's Auxiliary founded. Miss Anne McCormick hosts first meeting and is elected first president of the auxiliary.

— The Rev. J. Harold Wolf elected president of board.

1930 — The Parker Home is renovated to accomodate two more guests.

— Harry S. Keeney begins 14-year term as president of the board.

1931 — Clarion Presbytery joins corporation.

1932 — S. Sharpe Huston begins thirty years work as treasurer of the corporation.

1933 — William T. Swaim, Jr., elected a trustee of Presbyterian Home of Central Pennsylvania.

— Mrs. Parker sells former orphanage in Carlisle to Presbyterian Home of Central Pennsylvania for one gold dollar.

1934 — The Parker Annex opens in Carlisle, housing for eleven more guests.

— Swaim is named secretary of the board of trustees and of the executive committee. He becomes *de facto* administrator of both homes and of the corporation.

— Mrs. W.W. Heidelbaugh elected president of the women's auxiliary.

1936 — First issue of The Newville Home News distributed.

1938 — The Andrews Home opens in Newville.

— Plan for putting "Small, Scattered, Home-like Homes for the Aging first enunciated in speech by Bill Swaim at Tenth Anniversary celebration of The Parker Home.

1939 — Board approves plan for building The Farm Annex on Parker Farm.

— Mrs. Ira Henderson elected auxiliary president.

1940 — Bill Swaim named full-time administrator of Presbyterian Home of Central Pennsylvania

1941 — The Manor (originally The Farm Annex) opens. First home built by the corporation and largest to date. Housing for 21 guests.

1943 — Mrs. B.E.P. Prugh elected auxiliary prsident.

1944 — William S. Middleton, Esq., elected president of board of trustees.

1945 — Court rules that Presbyterian Home of Central Pennsylvania need not open an orphanage to satisfy terms of the Parker Will.

1947 — Mrs. E.S. Manning elected president of women's auxiliary.

1948 — Addition to The Parker Annex completed. Seven rooms added.

1949 — Mrs. J. Claire McCullough elected president of women's auxiliary.

1951 — The Hazleton Home opens. Marks first expansion of corporation outside of Carlisle Presbytery.

1952 — Hazleton Cottage opens.

1953 — Drive to remove restrictive language from charter begins.

— Mrs. J. Vance Thompson elected president of the women's auxiliary.

1954 — Chester Presbytery admitted to corporation. Promises to open home in lieu of admission fee.

— W. McConkey Kerr elected president of the board of trustees.

1955 — The Kennett Square Home opens.

1957 — Mrs. William S. Middleton elected president of the women's auxiliary.

1958 — The Mount Joy Home opens.

1960 — Rules change allows admission of male guests in some homes.

1961 — Mary Brower elected president of the women's auxiliary.

1962 — Charter undergoes major revision to remove all restrictive language about race and religion of guests. (see Appendix I. for text of revision.)

— Name of corporation changed to Presbyterian Homes of Central Pennsylvania.

— Milton H. Ranck elected president of the board of trustees.

— Capital Fund Drive begins. John D. Killian, Esq., is chairman. Mrs. Mamie Doud Eisenhower is honorary chairman.

1963 — First male resident ever to live in a Presbyterian Homes of Central Pennsylvania home moves into Hazelton Home.

1964 — The Kittaning Home opens.

— Albert L. Schartner begins work as assistant administrator of Presbyterian Homes of Central Pennsylvania.

1965 — The Rev. Frederick B. Crane elected president of the board of trustees.

— Mrs. J.W. Heisey elected president of the women's auxiliary.

1966 — The Williamsport Home, the last home built solely as a residential facility, opens.

1967 — Presbyterian Apartments, Inc., opens in Harrisburg.

— John D. Killian, Esq. elected president of the board of trustees.

1968 — The Andrews Home closes.

1969 — Bill Swaim retires after more than 36 years service with Presbyterian Homes of Central Pennsylvania.

— Mary Brower re-elected president of the women's auxiliary.

1970 — Albert Schartner begins work as administrator of the corporation.

— The Mount Joy Home opens nursing wing.

— Donald M. Carroll, Jr., elected president of the board of trustees.

1971 — Stephen Proctor hired as administrator of The Mount Joy Home.

— John D. Killian re-elected president of the board of trustees.

— Mrs. Paul Waugaman elected president of the women's auxiliary.

1972 — Forest Park Health Center purchased by Presbyterian Homes of Central Pennsylvania. Marks first nursing home owned and operated by the corporation.

— Geneva House, Inc., opens in Scranton. Fulfills promise of putting homes in each constituent presbytery.

— The Presbyterian Homes News suspends publication after 36 years to coordinate all mailings for capital funds drive.

— Capital fund drive begins with Howard Hunsworth as chairman. Mrs. Mamie Doud Eisenhower again serves as honorary chairman. (see 1962)

— Sycamore Manor, the largest nursing home owned by the corporation, opens. Provides care for 123 patients after additions completed in 1976.

1973 — Lehigh Manor nursing home purchased by corporation.

— Hazleton Cottage closes after 21 years.

— Howard Hunsworth elected president of the board of trustees.

1974 — Nursing wing at The Mount Joy Home closes.

— The Parker Home closes.

— Vernon Rigdon of Oxford named first vice president of finance.

1975 — Name of corporation changed to Presbyterian Homes, Inc.

— Non-Profit Services Associates, the consulting arm of Presbyterian Homes, Inc., organized.

— The Presbyterian Homes News resumes publication at conclusion of successful capital funds drive.

—Presbyterian Homes, Inc., begins graduate internship program for administrators in cooperation with North Texas State University.

— Mrs. John H.P. Strome elected president of the women's auxiliary.

1977 — Oxford Manor-The Steward Home, opens in Oxford. First nursing home built by the corporation. Land was the gift of John Ware, III. The new facility includes 100 nursing beds and 40 residential care units. Residential care wing, substantially funded by Dr. N.B. Steward, was the last residential care facility built by the corporation.

— Swaim Health Center opens in Newville. Marks first development at Newville property since the building of The Manor.

— The Kennett Square Home closes.

— Board of Trustees reorganized its officers. Howard Hunsworth, the last president of the board of trustees, was suceeded by the corporation's first chairman of the board, the Rev. Russell Weer. Albert Schartner, formerly the executive vice president, was named President and Chief Executive Officer.

1978 — Green Ridge Village apartments open. Cottage construction begins. Green Ridge Village is the first Continuing Care Campus opened by Presbyterian Homes, Inc. Mr. and Mrs. Jack Poorman establish the first trust fund for the endowment of Green Ridge Village.

— Presbyterian Homes, Inc., buys The Eliza Cathcart Home in Devon.

— Corporation marks 50th Anniversary.

— A. Gordon Turner elected chairman of the board of trustees.

— Jack Parson, C.P.A., named vice president of finance.

1979 — Hazleton Home closes.

— Stephen Proctor joins central office staff as the first vice president of operations.

— The Rev. Harry Farr elected chairman of the board of trustees.

— Mrs. Margaret O'Keefe elected president of the women's auxiliary.

1980 — PHI computer system goes on line bringing all data processing in house.

— The Rev. Lewis O. Paulhamus elected chairman of the board of trustees.

1981 — Work begins on Strategic Plan for corporation covering major goals and plans through the year 2000.

1982 — Nonprofit Services Associates, the consulting arm of Presbyterian Homes, Inc., is incorporated as Nonprofit Services Associates, Inc.

— A full-time Strategic Planner is added to the corporate staff.

1983 — Indiana Presbyterian Home opens. The land was donated by Julia Wilson Pound.

— Lehigh Manor renamed Westminster Village upon opening of Westminster House Apartments.

— Upper Ohio Valley Presbytery (incorporating southeastern Ohio and the northernmost sections of West Virginia) becomes the seventh cooperating presbytery with Presbyterian Homes, Inc.

— Mission statement revised (see Appendix I. for text)

— Robert Perry elected chairman of the board of trustees.

— Ronald Robinson, C.P.A., named vice president of finance.

— Mrs. John H.P. Strome elected convenor of the women's auxiliary. Beginning in 1983, each women's auxiliary became a seperate organization serving their local home. The convenor administrates an annual meeting for all auxiliary members from the various homes.

1984 — Community Home-Care Services was added to

work of Presbyterian Homes, Inc., with employment of June Hoffman, R.N. During 1984 offices opened in Harrisburg, Williamsport and Oxford.

— One West Penn, a 130-unit apartment complex opens in Carlisle.

— Presbyterian Homes, Inc., purchases Courtland Manor, a 100-bed nursing home in Dover, Delaware.

— Corporate central offices relocated from Dillsburg to 1217 Slate Hill Road, Camp Hill.

— Capital funds campaign begins in Kiskiminetas and Lehigh presbyteries.

— Vice President of Development added to staff with employment of the Rev. Peter Shultzabarger.

1985 — Maira Cleaver became the first woman elected chairman of the board of Presbyterian Homes, Inc.

— Construction began on The Woods at Oxford, at Mark H. Kennedy Park, St. Clairsville, Ohio, and at Green Ridge Village. All are Independent Living Units.

— Community Home-Care Services opens offices in Carlisle, Pennsylvania and in Wheeling, West Virginia.

# APPENDIX I.

The original charter as recorded in the Court of Common Pleas of Cumberland County is reproduced on the following pages. The document was transcribed rather than reproduced for the sake of clarity. After the original charter, the major amendments to the charter in 1962 which removed the limiting language from the purposes of the corporation are also transcribed. Both documents are on file in the courthouse in Carlisle, Pennsylvania. Copies are maintained at Presbyterian Homes, Inc., corporate offices in Camp Hill.

The third change of the corporate name, to Presbyterian Homes, Inc., occurred in 1975. Other amendments to the charter occurred at various times during the years of the corporation's history to change the number of board members with the addition of new constituent presbyteries. The most significant changes, excepting the most recent name change noted above, came in 1962 as the result of years of meetings and compromise on the part of the trustees and the presbyteries they represented. The newest mission statement, revised in 1983, represents the latest refining of the original charter. That statement is printed below. Exact information about changes in other years is a matter of public record in the Cumberland County Court of Common Pleas.

## Mission Statement
### revised 1983

The mission of Presbyterian Homes, Inc., is to offer Christian understanding, compassion, and a sense of belonging to those whose needs may be physical, psychological, social, financial, or spiritual in nature, by providing a full range of high quality health care, housing and other related community services directed primarily for the elderly which contribute to wholeness of body, mind, and spirit.

89

NO. 12359
CHARTER
COURT OF COMMON PLEAS
TO
PRESBYTERIAN HOME OF CENTRAL PA
DATED DEC. 14, 1926
ENTD. JAN. 12, 1927

In the Court of Common Pleas of Cumberland County, Pennsylvania.

No. 53 February Term, 1927.

To the Honorable E. M. Biddle, Jr., President and Sole Judge of said Court:

The undersigned, all of whom are citizens of Pennsylvania, having associated themselves together for the purpose of organization the Presbyterian Home of Central Pennsylvania, and being desirous of becoming incorporated agreeably to the provisions of the Act of Assembly entitled "An Act to provide for the incorporation and regulation of certain corporations," approved April 29, 1874, and the supplements thereto, do hereby certify:

1. The name of the proposed corporation is "Presbyterian Home of Central Pennsylvania."

2. The said corporation is formed for the purpose of the care of those people of the Presbyterian denomination hereinafter designated, namely, aged white people, dependent white children, and convalescent white children.

3. The business of the said corporation is to be transacted at Newville, Cumberland County, Pennsylvania.

4. The said Corporation is to exist perpetually.

5. The names and residences of the subscribers are as follows:

| Name | Residence |
|------|-----------|
| Glenn M. Shafer | Carlisle, PA |
| Ellen A. Parker | Carlisle, PA |
| Walter Stuart | Carlisle, PA |
| John S. Elliott | Newville, PA |
| Harry W. Keeny | Harrisburg, PA |

6. Future members are to be chosen by such body or in such manner as may be proscribed by the by-laws.

7. The said corporation shall be managed by a Board of Trustees consisting of twenty-one members, and the names and residences of those chosen for the first year as such Trustees are as follows:

| Name of Trustee | Residence |
|---|---|
| Ellen A. Parker | Carlisle, PA |
| Walter K. Sharpe | Chambersburg, PA |
| John S. Elliott | Newville, PA |
| Edward Bailey | Harrisburg, PA |
| Harry W. Keeny | Harrisburg, PA |
| Charles Rommel | Shippensburg, PA |
| Frank T. Wheeler | Newville, PA |
| David H. Johnston | Scranton, PA |
| Ebenezer E. Flack | Kingston, PA |
| O.R. Conrad | Scranton, PA |
| Luther S. Black | Easton, PA |
| Ernest Hansel | Ashland, PA |
| F.G.W. Runk | Allentown, PA |
| J. Harold Wolf | Mt. Carmel, PA |
| F.P. Everitt | Lewisburg, PA |
| George Hackett | Sunbury, PA |
| Harry W. Haring | Lancaster, PA |
| T. Edwin Redding | Stewartstown, PA |
| W.M. Workman | Mt. Joy, PA |
| Glenn M. Shafer | Carlisle, PA |

8. The said corporation has no capital stock. Witness our hands and seals this 14th day of December, 1926.

| | |
|---|---|
| Glenn M. Shaffer | (seal) |
| Ellen A. Parker | (seal) |
| W. Stuart | (seal) |
| J. S. Elliott | (seal) |
| Harry W. Keeny | (seal) |

STATE OF PENNSYLVANIA
COUNTY OF CUMBERLAND

Before me, the subscriber, personally appeared Glenn M. Shafer, Ellen A. Parker and Walter Stuart, all of whom are subscribers to the above and foregoing Certificate of Incorporation and in due form of law acknowledged the said Certificate to be their and each of their act and deed.

Witness my hand and notarial seal this 14th day of December, 1926.

T. Ralph Jacobs,
Notary Public,
Commission expires Feb. 3, 1929.

PROOF OF PUBLICATION   PROOF OF PUBLICATION
VALLEY-TIMES STAR          EVENING SENTINEL

STATE OF PENNSYLVANIA
COUNTY OF CUMBERLAND

W. Stuart being duly sworn, doth depose and say; That he is one of the corporators of the Presbyterian Home of Central Pennsylvania and that all of the subscribers to the foregoing certificate of incorporation are citizens of the State of Pennsylvania:

That said notice was publicized to wit:

In the Valley-Times Star on the 18th, 23rd and 30th days of December, 1926.

In the Evening Sentinel on the 18th, 23rd and 30th days of December, 1923.

Sworn to and subscribed before me, this 10th day of January 1927.

T. Ralph Jacobs    T.R.J.
Notary Public,    N.P.
Commission expires Feb. 3, 1929.


ORDER OF COURT

And now, January 11th, 1927, the within charter and certificate of incorporation with the proper certificate of registration attached as required by the Act of May 16, 1923, P.L. 246 having remained on file in the office of the Prothonotary of this Court since the 14th day of December,

1926, as appears by the record, I do hereby certify that I have examined and perused the said writing and have found the same to be in proper form and contain the purposes named in the first class specified in Section 2 of the Act of the General Assembly of the Commonwealth of Pennsylvania, entitled "An Act to provide for the Incorporation and regulation of certain corporations," approved April 29, 1874, and the supplements thereto, and the same appearing to be lawful and not injurious to the community, I do hereby, on motion of T. Ralph Jacobs, Esq., on behalf of the petitioners, order and direct that the said charter of

PRESBYTERIAN HOME OF CENTRAL PENNSYLVANIA aforesaid be and the same is hereby approved, and that upon the recording of the same and of this order, the subscribers thereto and their associates shall be a corporation by the name

PRESBYTERIAN HOME OF CENTRAL PENNSYLVANIA for the purposes and upon the terms therein stated.

By the Court,
E.M. Biddle, Jr.,
P.J.

OFFICE OF THE
SECRETARY OF THE COMMONWEALTH
OF PENNSYLVANIA
Harrisburg, December 15, 1926.

PENNSYLVANIA

I do hereby certify, that the name, title or designation "Presbyterian Home of Central Pennsylvania" was this day filed and recorded in this office as the title of a proposed corporation of the first class in accordance with the provisions of the Act entitled "An Act to provide for the registration and protection of names, titles or designations of associations, societies, orders, foundations, federations, organizations and corporations, of the first class," approved May 16th, 1923, and that a search of the records of this office fails to disclose any conflict between the aforesaid title and any other name, title or designation heretofore registered under the provision of the said Act.

In testimony whereof, I have hereunto set my hand and caused the seal of the Secretary's Office to be affixed, the day and year above written.

Geo. D. Thorn
Deputy Secretary of the Commonwealth.

IN RE: AMENDMENT OF ARTICLES
OF PRESBYTERIAN HOME OF
CENTRAL PENNSYLVANIA
IN THE COURT OF COMMON PLEAS OF
CUMBERLAND COUNTY, PENNSYLVANIA
NO. 53 FEBRUARY TERM, 1927

DECREE

AND NOW, this 31st day of May, 1962, upon presentation of the petition of PRESBYTERIAN HOME OF CENTRAL PENNSYLVANIA, together with a certified copy of the notice of meeting, resolution of membership, proofs of publication and the Certificate of Registration of the Department of State of the Commonwealth of Pennsylvania setting forth the availability of the name PRESBYTERIAN HOMES OF CENTRAL PENNSYLVANIA, and upon consideration of the same, the Court having found the Articles of Amendment to be in proper form, to be within the provisions of the Nonprofit Corporation Law of the Commonwealth of Pennsylvania, to be lawful, beneficial and not injurious to the community, on motion of Thomas I. Myers and Paul E. Clouser, Attorneys for Petitioner, it is

ORDERED and DECREED that the Articles of Amendment of PRESBYTERIAN HOME OF CENTRAL PENNSYLVANIA are approved and granted and, upon recording thereof, together with this Decree, they shall become effective so as to constitute the charter of PRESBYTERIAN HOMES OF CENTRAL PENNSYLVANIA.

BY THE COURT:

_____
Judge

PRESBYTERIAN HOMES OF CENTRAL PENNSYLVANIA

ARTICLES OF AMENDMENT

## ARTICLE I — NAME

The name of the Corporation is Presbyterian Homes of Central Pennsylvania.

## ARTICLE II — PURPOSES

The purposes of the Corporation, to which all its resources and the exercise of its powers are dedicated, are to alleviate the distress and hardship of the aging and of minor children by ministering to the particular needs of these persons, and by this Christian witness to advance the Kingdom of God, promote social welfare, and lessen the burdens of government. The Corporation does not contemplate pecuniary gain or profit, incidental or otherwise, to its members.

## ARTICLE III — PRINCIPAL OFFICE

The principal office of the Corporation is Newville, Cumberland County, Pennsylvania.

## ARTICLE IV — TERM OF EXISTENCE

The Corporation is to exist perpetually.

## ARTICLE V — POWERS

The Corporation shall have the following powers, as limited, and in addition to those given, by the Laws of the Commonwealth of Pennsylvania:

A. To accept, acquire, receive, take, and hold by request, devise, grant, gift, purchase, exchange, lease, transfer, judicial order or decree, or otherwise, for any of its objects and purposes, any property, both real and personal, of whatever kind, nature, or description and wherever situated.

B. To sell, exchange, convey, mortgage, lease, transfer, or otherwise dispose of any property, either real or personal, the continued use or ownership of which the Trustees may determine is no longer necessary for the objects and purposes of the Corporation.

C. To borrow money, and, from time to time, to make, accept, endorse, execute, and issue bonds, debentures, promissory notes, bills of exchange and other obligations of the Corporation for moneys borrowed or in payment for property acquired or for any of the other purposes of the Corporation, and to secure the payment of any such obligations by mortgage, note, pledge, deed indenture, agreement, or other instrument of trust, or by other lien upon, assignment of, or agreement in regard to all or any part of the property, rights, or privileges of the corporation wherever situated, whether now owned or hereafter to be acquired.

D. To invest and reinvest its funds in such stocks, bonds, debentures, mortgages, or in such other securities and property as its Board of Trustees shall deem advisable, subject to the limitations and conditions contained in any request, devise, grant, or gift.

E. In general, to exercise such other powers which now are or hereafter may be conferred by law upon a Corporation organized for the purposes hereinabove set forth, or necessary of incidental to the powers so conferred, or conducive to the attainment of the purposes of the Corporation.

## ARTICLE VI — MEMBERSHIP

Membership in the corporation shall consist of those persons constituting the Board of Trustees at any particular time in accordance with the provisions of the By-laws and existing law.

## ARTICLE VII — MANAGEMENT

The business and affairs of the Corporation shall be managed by a Board of Trustees, which shall consist of three (3) members from, and elected by, each of those Presbyteries of the United Presbyterian Church in the U.S.A. within the State of Pennsylvania cooperating with and rendering financial support to the Corporation together with six members-at-large as elected by the Board of Trustees in accordance with the By-Laws.

## ARTICLE VIII — NON-STOCK BASIS

The Corporation is organized upon a non-stock basis.

## ARTICLE IX — AMENDMENT OF ARTICLES

Amendments of these Articles shall be effected as provided by law and in addition thereto shall be approved by a majority of those Presbyteries of the United Presbyterian Church in the U.S.A. within the State of Pennsylvania, cooperating with and rendering financial support to the Corporation.

## ARTICLE X — DISSOLUTION

In the event of dissolution, other than by merger or consolidation with a similar charitable or religious entity, the assets of the Corporation, whether in cash or in kind, shall be distributed as determined by the Board of Trustees to the then participating presbytery of the United Presbyterian Church in the U.S.A. to be used for the same or comparable purposes set forth in Article II hereof.

# APPENDIX II.

The men and women who began the work of Presbyterian Homes, Inc., met in small committees throughout the Presbyteries which banded together to form the original corporation. The list that follows traces the founders through 1932 when S. Sharpe Huston began his thirty years of service as treasurer of the corporation. The list was compiled by William T. Swaim, Jr., in 1938 for the Tenth Anniversary celebration of The Parker Home and of the corporation.

## TRUSTEES
of Early Committees and the Board of Trustees of the Home

### 1920-1938

Prepared by Rev. Wm. T. Swaim, Jr., for Tenth Anniversary of the Parker Home, Newville, Pennsylvania.

REV. J. HAROLD WOLF, Mount Carmel, PA
Father of the Presbyterian Home

Session of Mount Carmel Church sent recommendation to Northumberland Presbytery.

INVESTIGATING COMMITTEE APPOINTED BY NORTH-UMBERLAND PRESBYTERY September, 1920.

Rev. J. Harold Wolf
Rev. E.C. Armstrong, D.D.
Rev. A.H. Hibschman, D.D., Milton
Elder Jas. B. Graham
Elder George Hackett, Sunbury

99

Added in September, 1922
Rev. T.M. Hurst
Elder Sidney T. Furst, Lock Haven
Elder R.A. McCachran, Bloomsburg
Elder H.L. Bond, Lewisburg

December 21, 1922
Rev. F.B. Everitt of Lewisburg took the place of Rev. A.H. Hibschman, D.D.

1923 — Added to the Committee
Elder J.N. Glover
Elder George C. Chapin

1923
Dr. Armstrong visited Lehigh Presbytery.

Rev. Frank B. Everitt visited the Presbyteries of Philadelphia and Westminster.

1924
Dr. Gilland and Mr. McCullagh were released from the Investigating Committee.

Added to the Committee:
Rev. E.C. Granger, D.D., Williamsport
Elder David L. Glover, Esq., Mifflinburg

March 10, 1925 — Meeting of Committeemen from Presbyteries, Sunbury, PA

Carlisle Presbytery — Dr. George E. Hawes and Elder Harry W. Keeny
Huntingdon Presbytery — Elder James S. Woods, Esq.
Lackawanna Presbytery — Rev. D.H. Johnston, D.D.
Lehigh Presbytery — Rev. Ernest Hansel, Ashland
Northumberland Presbytery — Revs. J.H. Wolf, F.B. Everitt and E.C. Armstrong; Elders H.L. Bond and J.N. Glover
Clarion Presbytery — Invited, but sent no delegates
Westminster Presbytery — Invited, but sent no delegates

Rev. J. Harold Wolf, Chairman
Rev. F.B. Everitt, Secretary

Sub-committee to interview Mrs. Harrison about broadening scope of offer to include crippled children — Rev. D.H. Johnston, D.D., and elders H.W. Keeny and H.L. Bond.

Sub-committee to draft a Permanent Plan for Co-operation — Elder Jas. S. Woods, Esq., Rev. R.C. Walker and Rev. Geo. Hawes, D.D.

September, 1925
Northumberland Presbytery's Committee Revised to include:
Rev. J.H. Wolf
Rev. Frank B. Everitt
Rev. E.C. Armstrong, D.D.
Rev. T.M. Hurst
REv. C.E. Granger, D.D.
Elder H.L. Bond
Elder J.N. Glover
Elder D.L. Glover, Esq.
Elder Geo. Hackett
Elder Geo. Diack
Elder H.W. Kries

Presbyteries Visited:
Carlisle Presbytery — Rev. J.H. Wolf and Elder H.W. Keeny
Clarion Presbytery — Rev. T.M. Hurst
Huntingdon Presbytery — Rev. J.H. Wolf and Rev. F.B. Everitt
Lackawanna Presbytery — Rev. F.B. Everitt
Lehigh Presbytery — Rev. F.B. Everitt (dinner conference)
Westminster Presbytery — Rev. F.B. Everitt and Elder Harry W. Keeny

1925 — The First Official Representatives of the Presbyteries
Carlisle —
Clarion —

Huntingdon — 3/9/26 withdrew, as were already committed to the Dysart Home at Hollidaysburg

Lackawanna — Rev. Ebenezer Flack, D.D., Kingston, and Rev. D.H. Johnston, D.D.

Northumberland — (see above)

Lehigh — Rev. Ernest Hansel, Rev. L.S. Black, Easton, and Elder F.G.W. Runk, Allentown

Westminster — Rev. H.W. Haring, D.D., Rev. T. Edwin Redding, Stewartstown, and Elder William M. Workman, M.D., Mount Joy


November 10-11, 1925

Persons Present at the First Joint Meeting of the Orphanage Committee of the Seven Central Pennsylvania Presbyteries.

Lewisburg, PA

Clarion — Augustus Luft, Coudersport

Lehigh — Rev. E. Hansel, Chm.; Rev. L.S. Black, Rev. H.S. Welty, Hokendauqua, and Elder F.G.W. Runk

Carlisle — Rev. J.L. Conrow, D.D., Chm., Greencastle; Rev. Glenn M. Shafer, D.D., Carlisle, and Elders H.W. Keeny, Harrisburg, and C.W. Hunt, Camp Hill.

Westminster — Rev. H.W. Haring, D.D., Chm., Lancaster; Rev. T. Edwin Redding and Elder Wm. M. Workman, M.D.

Northumberland — Rev. H.J. Wolf, Chm.; Rev. F.B. Everitt, Rev. E.C. Armstrong of Williamsport; Rev. T.M. Hurst, Arnot; Elders Geo. Hackett, H.L. Bond, D.L. Glover and H.W. Krise, Milton.


Other Names that appear on Committees appointed:

Rev. Henry B. Strock, D.D., Clarion Presbytery

Elder R.H. Somerville (Huntingdon)

W.K. Woodbury, Esq., Pottsville, Lehigh

Rev. Walter Hogue, D.D., York, Westminster

Rev. Dr. Reeves (Huntingdon)

Rev. H.F. Earseman (Clarion)

F.E. Parkhurst, Wilkes-Barre, Lackawanna

Rev. Dr. Miller (Huntingdon)

Elder H.C. Jackson (Westminster)

Rev. Dr. Bell (Clarion)

Rev. J. Leonard Hynson, Lebanon
Elder C.D. Osterhout (Clarion)
Elder Otto Conrad (Lackawanna)
Rev. Dr. Francis (Huntingdon)


March 9, 1926
Second Joint Meeting of the Orphanage Committee of the
Central Pennsylvania Presbyteries
Sunbury, PA
Carlisle — Rev. Glenn Shafer, D.D., and Elder H.W. Keeny
Clarion — Rev. J.V. Bell, D.D., and Augustus Luft
Lackawanna — Revs. E. Flack, D.D., and D.H. Johnston,
D.D., and Otto Conrad
Lehigh — Revs. E. Hansel and H.S. Welty and Elder F.G.W.
Runk
Northumberland — Revs. J.H. Wolf, F.B. Everitt, E.C.
Armstrong, D.D., T.M. Hurst and E.D. Parkhill and Elders
H.L. Bond, Geo. Hackett and J.N. Glover
Westminster — Rev. T.E. Redding


June 14, 1926
Third Joint Meeting of the Orphanage Committee
Harrisburg, PA
Carlisle — Rev. G.M. Shafer and Elders C.W. Hunt and
H.W. Keeny
Lackawanna — Revs. E. Flack and D.H. Johnston
Lehigh — Revs. E. Hansel, L.S. Black and H.S. Welty and
Elder Funk
Northumberland — Revs. J.H. Wolf, F.B. Everitt, E.C.
Armstrong and Elders D.L. Glover, J.N. Glover and Geo.
Hackett
Westminster — Revs. H.W. Haring and T.E. Redding
Clarion — Not Represented


Elder B.F. Williams, Emlenton, succeeded L.L. Strock of
Chm. of Clarion


Elder VanDusen Rickert, Pottsville, succeeded W.K.
Woodbury, Lehigh

At this meeting, "The thanks of the Committee were also extended to the officers of the Committee for their untiring work in prosecuting this matter to such a successful conclusion."

November 16, 1926
First Meeting of the Duly Elected Representatives of the Board of Governors of the five co-operating Presbyteries
Harrisburg
Carlisle — Elders H.W. Keeny and Chas. Rommel, Shippensburg
Lackawanna — Rev. D.H. Johnston, D.D.
Lehigh — Revs. L.S. Black and Ernest Hansel and Elder F.G.W. Runk
Northumberland — Revs. J.H. Wolf, F.B. Everitt and Elder George Hackett
Westminster — Revs. H.W. Haring, D.D., T.E. Redding, and Dr. Wm. M. Workman
Parker Trustees — Rev. Glenn M. Shafer, Mrs. Ellen A. Parker, Carlisle and John S. Elliott, Newville
Temporary Organization:
Rev. Glenn M. Shafer, D.D., Chairman
Rev. F.B. Everitt, Secretary
February 1, 1927
Meeting for setting up Permanent Organization
Harrisburg
Carlisle — Rev. F.T. Wheeler, Newville, Elders H.W. Keeny and Chas. Rummell
Lackawanna — Rev. E. Flack, D.D.
Lehigh — Rev. E. Hansel, Rev. L.S. Black and F.G.W. Runk, Esq.
Northumberland — Rev. J.H. Wolf, Rev. F.B. Everitt and Elder Geo. Hackett
Westminster — Rev. H.W. Haring, D.D., Rev. T.E. Redding and Dr. Workman
Members-at-large — Rev. Glenn M. Shafer, Mrs. Ellen Parker, Jn. S. Elliott and Walter Stuart
Absentees — Rev. D.H. Johnston, O.R. Conrad, Walter Sharpe and Edward Bailey
President — Dr. Shafer

1st V.P. — Rev. J.H. Wolf
2nd V.P. — Fred G.W. Runk
Secretary — Rev. F.B. Everitt
Treasurer — Walter Stuart, Carlisle
Finance Committee — Dr. Haring; and Messrs. Hackett, Bailey and Runk
Building Committee — Mr. Keeny, Chm., Mrs. Parker and Revs. Redding, Hansel and Johnston
Rules and Admissions — Dr. Flack, Chm., Dr. Workman, Rev. L.S. Black, Mr. Conrad, Rummell
Executive Committee — Officers and Messrs, Jn. F. Elliott, Chas. L. Rummell and F.T. Wheeler

October 25, 1927
Resignations of Walter Sharpe and J.S. Elliott were accepted. Mr. Keeny was elected to the Executive committee succeeding Mr. John S. Elliott.

January 24, 1928
The five officers were re-elected, together with Messrs. Wheeler, Keeny and Rummell as the Executive Committee.

April 24, 1928
D.L. Glover, Esq. of Mifflinburg and W. McConkey Kerr of York were elected as Members-at-large, succeeding Messrs. Jn. S. Elliott and Walter Sharpe. F.B. Pomeroy of Troy succeeded O.R. Conrad, Lackawanna, resigned.

October 4, 1928
Dr. Walter W. Edge of Lancaster elected, succeeding Dr. Haring, resigned.

January 22, 1929
Mr. Edward Bailey resigned as a Trustee of the Home, after buying dinner for the Board.

ELECTION OF OFFICERS
(Dr. Shafer refused re-election because of his new work as Clerk of Synod.)
President — Rev. J. Harold Wolf

First Vice President — Rev. Franklin T. Wheeler
Second Vice President — F.G.W. Runk
Secretary — Rev. F.B. Everitt
Treasurer — Walter Stuart
Executive Committee — Messrs. Wolf. Everitt, Wheeler, Keeny, Kerr and Shafer (ex-officio)

**April 23, 1929**
Rev. Peter K. Emmons, D.D., elected to succeed Rev. D.H. Johnston, D.D. Elder Theodore L. Welles, First Church, Wilkes-Barre, to succeed F.B. Pomeroy

**June 16, 1929**
Miss Anne McCormick, Harrisburg, elected Trustee-at-Large, succeeding Mr. Edward Bailey.

**October 22, 1929**
Rev. W.G. Finney attended his first meeting, succeeding Rev. F.B. Everitt. Rev. F.B. Everitt resigned as Secretary of the Board of Trustees. Harry W. Keeny was elected Secretary of the Board of Trustees. George Hackett was elected a member of the Executive Committee, as Mr. Keeny moved up.

**January 28, 1930**
ELECTION OF OFFICERS
President — Harry W. Keeny
First Vice President — Rev. Franklin T. Wheeler
Second Vice President — F.G.W. Runk, Esq.
Secretary — Rev. T. Edwin Redding
Treasurer — Walter Stuart
Executive Committee — Messrs. Keeny, Redding, Wolf, Wheeler, Hackett and Shafer

April 29, 1930
Elder C.A. Battenburg, Scranton, succeeding Elder Theodore L. Welles.

June 24, 1930
Rev. C.H. Russell, Plymouth, attended, succeeding Rev. Peter K. Emmons, resigned.

October 25, 1930
Dr. Flack, though not a member, met with the Executive Committee.

January 27, 1931
ELECTION OF OFFICERS
First Trustees from Clarion Presbytery
Elder J.W. Boyd Allison (present at April 28th meeting of Board), Punxsutawney
Elder J.C. Craig, Rimersburg
Rev. J. Vernon Bell, D.D.

October 27, 1931
Rev. Harry T. Chisholm, D.D., elected to succeed Rev. J. Vernon Bell, D.D., deceased.

January 26, 1932
ELECTION OF OFFICERS
100% re-election of officers (see Jan. 27, 1931 and Jan. 28, 1930, above)

May 17, 1932
Mr. Walter Stuart resigned as a Trustee and as Treasurer of the Board of Trustees. Mr. S. Sharpe Huston, Carlisle, was elected to succeed Mr. Walter Stuart as Treasurer. (All Funds were transferred from the Farmers Trust Co. to the Carlisle Trust Co.)

# APPENDIX III.

In this section we will list the various homes, services, and subsidiary corporations that together constitute Presbyterian Homes, Inc. Each is listed in the order of their opening. The dates listed included the opening year and the closing year for those facilities no longer in operation.

In every case, the first official name of the facility is listed in the name line. If the present name is different, the change is noted in the text and the latest name is listed in parentheses below the original name. Underneath the name, address, and dates of the various homes is a note mentioning the type of facility that home was or is. These types break down as follows:

1. **A Residential Home** provides three meals per day and private rooms for each person living in the home. Residents of these facilities need no continuing medical care and are, for the most part, ambulatory. Residential care was the sole type of care provided by Presbyterian Homes of Central Pennsylvania from 1928 through 1970.

2. **Independent Living Units** (ILUs) describes another level of care offered by Presbyterian Homes, Inc. ILUs can be apartments or cottages and can be part of a larger facility or stand alone. The difference between ILUs operated by Presbyterian Homes, Inc. and is in the resident's neighbors. The apartments and cottages are the same kinds of facilities one would find in any modern apartment complex or housing development. The first apartments opened in 1967. The first cottages opened in 1978.

3. **Nursing Homes** provide round-the-clock care for patients with chronic illnesses that prevent them from living independently. Nursing homes that are part of Presbyterian Homes, Inc., first opened in 1970 and now are the largest single type of care provided by the corporation.

4. **Continuing Care Campuses** combine two or three levels of care on the same grounds or within the same building. The first continuing care campus opened in 1973.

5. **Community Home-Care Services** provides routine nursing services to patients with acute or with chronic illnesses who are still able to live at home. The first Community Home Care Services office opened in January of 1984.

6. **Nonprofit Services Associates, Inc.,** is the consulting arm of Presbyterian Homes, Inc.

The inclusion of the Parker Farm as a separate listing is the result of its place in the history of Presbyterian Homes, Inc. Each of the facilities on the Parker Farm are listed separately.

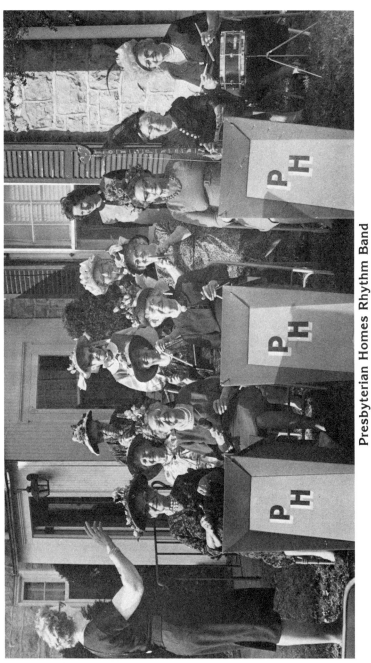

Presbyterian Homes Rhythm Band

The Parker Home

# The Parker Home
# Big Spring Road
# Newville, Pennsylvania
# 1928-1974*
# A Residential Home

The Parker Home opened on September 17, 1928, as the first Presbyterian Home of Central Pennsylvania. Mrs. Ellen Ard Parker donated the farmhouse and 93 acres of land to the original corporation in the name of her late husband, William Henderson Parker. The Parker Home remained open until 1974 when government-mandated modifications to the building made the home too expensive to continue in operation.

Today the Parker Home serves as a conference center and a retreat house for Presbyterian Homes, Inc. The building also serves as a continuing reminder of the generosity of Mrs. Parker and of the founders of Presbyterian Homes, Inc. The Parker Home is located on the continuing care campus now known as Green Ridge Village. The Parker Home housed nine guests at its opening and was expanded to provide a home for a total of eleven guests in 1930.

*This date indicates the closing of the facility as a home for the aging. The building, as noted in the text, is still used for conferences and as a retreat house.

The Parker Farm

# The Parker Farm
# Big Spring Road
# Newville, Pennsylvania
# 1928-

The Parker Farm was part of the original bequest that included the farmhouse listed above as The Parker Home. The Parker Farm provided the site for The Farm Annex (renamed The Manor shortly after it opened) in 1940, the Swaim Health Center in 1977, and Green Ridge Village (which includes all the homes just listed plus apartments and cottages known as Independent Living Units).

The land was actively farmed until 1962 both by tenant farmers and by employees of the corporation. In 1962 plans were approved for reforestation of some of the farm with pine trees and for the sale of some of the farm acreage to neighboring farmers. Because Mrs. Parker's estate came to the corporation over two decades rather than all at once, the farm included as many as 256 acres and presently includes less than 100 acres.

Though farming never made much money as an enterprise, the tradition lasted until the last sheep were sold in 1962. The Green Ridge Village property is now circled by trees, but neighboring farms continue to give the property the country feeling of first years of The Parker Home.

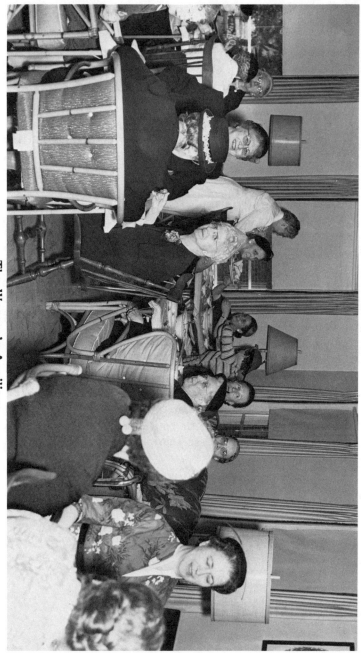

The Women's Auxiliary

# The Women's Auxiliary
# 1929-

The Women's Auxiliary has no central address. It's address is the address of every home listed in this section —past, present, and future. Until 1983, the women's auxiliary had an elected president who served as an ex-officio member of the board of trustees and of the executive committee of the board.

That the auxiliary now has no central administration reflects the history of their work. Throughout the history of the corporation, the women's auxiliary has met needs in the individual homes that the treasury would not stretch to cover, and, in many cases, needs that the administration missed. It was the women's auxiliary who raised the money during the first years of the depression to buy the first electric refrigerator used by The Parker Home.

Members of the auxiliary have arranged for painting and decorating rooms for guests too shy to make their request directly. They take individual residents to their homes for holidays and for birthdays. They have brightened parlors, furnished rooms, donated decorations, and done the thousands of small and large tasks that mean so much to the men and women who live in Presbyterian Homes, Inc., facilities.

The first meeting of the women's auxiliary was held in the summer home of Miss Anne McCormick of Harrisburg on September 13, 1929—just a year after the first home opened. Their service since has been an unbroken record of selfless giving. They represent the spirit of Presbyterian Homes, Inc., at its best. The quotation that opens the book is repeated at the top of this section because, while it speaks of the work of the entire corporation in a general sense, it speaks of the individual work of each member of the women's auxiliary in particular.

Carlisle Presbyterian Home

# The Parker Annex
# (Carlisle Presbyterian Home)
# 602 North Hanover Street
# Carlisle, Pennsylvania
# 1934-
# A Residential Home

Now known as the Carlisle Presbyterian Home, the Parker Annex opened in 1934 as the second Presbyterian Home of Central Pennsylvania. This home, like the first, was a gift of Mrs. Ellen Ard Parker. The home was originally built as an orphanage housing 20 children and run by Mrs. Parker from 1911 - 1915 when ill health compelled her to close the facility.

Mrs. Parker's gift of this home said the property could be sold at any time to expand the facilities on the Parker Farm. Instead, the Parker Annex was expanded in the late 1940s and remains open today. The location of the Parker Annex changed the direction of Presbyterian Homes of Central Pennsylvania for the next 35 years. William T. Swaim, Jr., who became secretary of the board of trustees and de facto administrator of the two homes at about the same time the Parker Annex opened, noticed that prospective guests favored the Parker Annex over the Parker Farm. The reason was the Parker Annex's downtown location.

Swaim's experience in these early years would lead to Presbyterian Home of Central Pennsylvania buying and building homes with downtown addresses almost exclusively from 1950 through 1970. The Parker Annex housed 11 guests at its opening and was expanded to house seven more guests in 1948.

The Andrews Home

# The Andrews Home
# 65 Big Spring Avenue
# Newville, Pennsylvania
# 1938-1968
# A Residential Home

The third home, like the first two homes, came to the Presbyterian Home of Central Pennsylvania from the generosity of a widow in memory of her husband, and in this case, also in memory of Mrs. Andrew's only daughter. The Andrews family used their Newville home as a summer house and lived in New York for the rest of the year. The Andrews Home has the dubious distinction as the first of the homes to close.

Like The Parker Home, government mandated structural changes made the home too expensive to continue in operation. The Andrews Home housed ten women and at it's opening raised the number of women cared for by the corporation to 31.

The Manor Home

# The Farm Annex
# (The Manor)
# (Manor Presbyterian Home)
# Big Spring Road
# Newville, Pennsylvania
# 1941-
# A Residential Home

Shortly after The Farm Annex opened it was renamed The Manor and the name remains today. The Farm Annex was the first Presbyterian Home of Central Pennsylvania that was built from the ground up. The Farm Annex was built on the Parker Farm in a cornfield opposite The Parker Home. From its opening it was the largest of the homes and remained so until 1964 when The Kittanning Home opened.

The work of building and opening this massive stone structure was a primary reason the trustees hired the first full-time administrator for the corporation, William T. Swaim, Jr., who had served as executive secretary and as part-time administrator for six years prior to his appointment.

The Manor houses 14 residents today. With the opening of this home, Presbyterian Home of Central Pennsylvania was home for 52 women. The Manor is now part of the continuing care campus known as Green Ridge Village located on the original Parker Farm property.

The Hazleton Home

# The Hazleton Home
# 126 North Church Street
# Hazleton, Pennsylvania
# 1951-1979
# A Residential Home

The Hazleton Home was the first Home purchased by the Presbyterian Home of Central Pennsylvania. The stone mansion also marked the corporation's first expansion outside Carlisle Presbytery. Located near the center of Hazleton, this home also confirms the plan of putting "Small, Scattered, Home-like, Homes for the Aging" in each of the six contributing presbyteries that made up the Presbyterian Home of Central Pennsylvania.

Built in 1924 by Mr. and Mrs. Calvin Pardee, Jr., the house was built of stone with 23-inch-thick walls, leaded glass windows in the solarium and other rooms, and it was located close to the center of Hazleton.

The Hazleton Home housed 18 guests until it closed in 1979. Its opening provided the momentum for expansion during the years that followed. The opening of this home meant Presbyterian Home of Central Pennsylvania now cared for 78 guests.

The Hazleton Cottage

# The Hazleton Cottage
# 217 W. Tamarack Street
# Hazleton, Pennsylvania
# 1952-1973
# A Residential Home

The Hazleton Cottage was actually the garage of the mansion that became The Hazleton Home. The garage was built with the same thick stone walls that were used in the mansion house. It was large enough to have a turntable for the family limosine, so its conversion to a small home was relatively easy.

Although The Hazleton Cottage housed only eight guests, it was very important to the expansion of the ministry of the Presbyterian Home of Central Pennsylvania. The Hazleton Cottage gave the corporation another address outside Carlisle Presbytery that helped to confirm their plans of eventually opening homes in all of the contributing presbyteries. One distinct advantage of the home was the entrance. The front door was built into the former garage door opening so no steps hindered the guests from coming or going. Three or four steps on a porch can be a significant barrier for persons in their seventies and older.

The small cottage fit well within the corporate plan to open small, scattered, homes for the aging and raised the total capacity of the homes to 84 guests in six facilities.

The Kennett Square Home

# The Kennett Square Home
# 319 North Lincoln Street
# Kennett Square, Pennsylvania
# 1955-1977
# A Residential Home

Opening The Kennett Square Home marked the opening of the seventh home in yet another presbytery. Chester Presbytery joined the first six contributing Presbyteries of Presbyterian Home of Central Pennsylvania in 1953. The opening of The Kennett Square Home was part of the arrangement made for the admission of Chester Presbytery to the corporation. Fees were discussed when serious negotiations began, but all parties agreed that if Chester Presbytery opened a home within their borders, no fee for admission to the corporation would be proper or necessary.

The Kennett Square Home housed 20 guests. It was eventually closed in 1977 because the opening of the Steward Home, on the Ware property would serve the needs of the area. Kennett Square also would have fallen victim to the ever more restrictive building codes that govern homes for the aging had it not closed when it did. The Kennett Square Home raised the number of residents cared for by the corporation to 108.

The Schock Presbyterian Home

# The Mount Joy Home
# (The Schock Home)
# (Schock Presbyterian Home)
# 37 West Main Street
# Mount Joy, Pennsylvania
# 1958-
# A Residential Home

The Mount Joy Home, later known as Schock Presbyterian Home in honor of the family that donated the building, was the last home to open during the 1950s. The opening of The Mount Joy Home also brought the corporation into four of the seven presbyteries that constituted the corporation.

In 1970 Schock Presbyterian Home was partially converted to provide skilled nursing care for 17 persons. The nursing facility was converted back to residential rooms five years after it opened due to government-mandated changes in the building, but the facility provided the corporation's first actual experience in providing nursing care. Today Schock Presbyterian Home houses 14 residents.

The building was built as the home of Clarence Schock, founder of SICO, Schock Independent Oil Company. The home is located very close to the center of Mount Joy. Part of the ministry of Schock Presbyterian Home is to provide, "Meals-on-Wheels" for older residents of the surrounding community. Residents are also active in the Mount Joy Senior Center which meets nearby. With the addition of the Schock Home, the eight units of Presbyterian Home of Central Pennsylvania housed 130 guests.

The Kittanning Presbyterian Home

# The Kittanning Home (Kittanning Presbyterian Home) 322 North McKean Street Kittanning, Pennsylvania 1964- A Residential Home

The Kittanning Home, now known as Kittanning Presbyterian Home, became the largest of the homes at its opening, providing a home for 24 guests. The Kittanning Home raised the number of homes to nine and the number of Presbyteries with homes to five. The Kittanning Home was the first new facility built by the corporation since the construction of The Manor in the late 1930s.

The Kittanning Home's downtown location continued the philosophy of locating "Small, Scattered, Home-Like Homes for the Aging" near the center of life in town. Today Kittanning Presbyterian Home is one of four of the ten original ten residential homes still in operation. The total capacity of the nine homes was 154.

The Williamsport Presbyterian Home

# The Williamsport Home (Williamsport Presbyterian Home) 810 Louisa Street Williamsport, Pennsylvania 1966- A Residential Home

The Williamsport Home, now known as Williamsport Presbyterian Home, is one of the most beautiful of all the homes. It is located on a spacious lot on a tree-lined street. It was built from stone with a slate roof and a rambling design that blends with the other buildings in the neighborhood.

The Williamsport Home is also the last independent residential care facility built by the corporation. The Steward Home, part of Oxford Manor, was built in 1977 as a residential care wing of the larger nursing facility, but Williamsport was the site of the last home built exclusively for residential care. Housing 24 residents, the facility brought residential homes to six of the seven contributing Presbyteries that constituted Presbyterian Homes of Central Pennsylvania. The opening of this home raised the capacity of the ten homes to a total of 178 residents.

**Presbyterian Apartments**

# Presbyterian Apartments, Inc. 322 North Second Street Harrisburg, Pennsylvania 1967- Apartments for the Aging

Presbyterian Apartments, Inc., houses more than 200 residents in 165 apartments in a 23-story structure located in downtown Harrisburg. Presbyterian Apartments, Inc., is a subsidiary corporation of Presbyterian Homes, Inc., with its own directors. Presbyterian Homes, Inc., provides administrative services for the complex through Nonprofit Services Associates, Inc., described later in this section.

Presbyterian Apartments, Inc., was built under a loan program sponsored by the Bureau of Housing and Urban Development (HUD). Residents of the apartment complex pay scaled rent based on financial need. Overall rents are based on the annual budget of the corporation.

The building is one of the largest in Harrisburg. It offers a view of miles of the Susquehanna Valley on clear days from the patios on the upper floors. The building was designed to allow replacement of all repairable service systems (water, electric, sewer, etc.) through accessible panels. All critical systems can be renovated and updated without structural work on the building. The building should serve the aging in Harrisburg long past the amortization of its 40-year mortgage. The sheer size of the building meant that the corporation housed more people in this apartment building than in all the residential homes combined once the apartments reached full occupancy.

The Ware Mansion

# Ware Presbyterian Village
# 7 Locust Street
# Oxford, Pennsylvania
# 1967-
# Apartments for the Aging

Ware Presbyterian Village is the basis of several projects of Presbyterian Homes, Inc. In 1967 seven apartments opened in the newly-renovated Ware Mansion. A gift of the Ware family, the property comprised the mansion itself and 13 acres near the center of Oxford. The renovated mansion housed 12 in seven apartments. The grounds of the Ware Mansion, like those of the Parker Farm, formed the basis for three later projects by Presbyterian Homes, Inc.

The first was Oxford Manor, a 100-bed nursing care facility, which opened in 1977 in the same building with the Steward Home, a 40-unit residential care facility. In 1985, construction began on the Woods cottages, an independent living development on the Ware Mansion grounds.

After the development of the Woods cottages, the Ware Mansion is to be renovated to provide a central recreation center for the residents of the independent living units. The Ware property, along with Green Ridge Village, Westminster Village, and Hutchinson House/Cathcart Home comprise the four continuing Care Campuses that are part of Presbyterian Homes, Inc.

Geneva House Apartments

# Geneva House, Inc.
# 323 Adams Avenue
# Scranton, Pennsylvania
# 1972-
# Apartments for the Aging

Geneva House, Inc., opened in 1972 as the fulfillment of a 34-year-old promise made by the trustees of Presbyterian Home of Central Pennsylvania to provide care for the elderly in each of their constituent presbyteries. Two attempts were made by the trustees to start a residential home in Scranton during the late 1950s and mid-1960s. These homes, had they opened, would have provided housing for residents. The nine-story Geneva House apartment building houses more than 130 residents in 105 apartments.

Like Presbyterian Apartments, Inc., Geneva House, Inc., was funded by the Housing and Urban Development authority (HUD), and is constituted as a subsidiary corporation. With the opening of Geneva House, coupled with the conversion of part of The Schock Home to a nursing facility, and the closing of The Newville Home, Presbyterian Homes of Central Pennsylvania housed less than 140 residents in nine homes, provided 16 nursing care beds in Mount Joy, and operated 277 apartments for the elderly in three facilities.

Forest Park Health Center

# Forest Park Health Center 700 Walnut Bottom Road Carlisle, Pennsylvania 1972- A Nursing Home

Although the renovated Mount Joy Presbyterian Home provided the first nursing care offered by Presbyterian Homes of Central Pennsylvania in 1970, Forest Park Health Center was the first nursing home in the Presbyterian Homes, Inc., system. Forest Park Health Center is located on the southwest side of Carlisle very near the new Second Presbyterian Church of Carlisle—the home church of Ellen A. Parker, the Rev. Glenn Shafer, Walter Stuart, and several other founders of Presbyterian Home of Central Pennsylvania. This location also puts Forest Park Health Center less than 15 miles from the first home—The Parker Home in Newville.

Forest Park Health Center was a 96-bed, for-profit nursing facility before it was acquired by Presbyterian Homes, Inc. It has since expanded to 100 beds with a new activities room. Several programs for the surrounding community, like meals-on-wheels and child day care were successfully initiated at Forest Park Health Center then adopted by other facilities. The opening of Forest Park Health Center increased the corporation's nursing care capacity to 112 beds.

Sycamore Manor Health Center

# Sycamore Manor
# Health Center
# 1445 Sycamore Road
# Montoursville, Pennsylvania
# 1972-
# A Nursing Home

Sycamore Manor Health Center was yet another acquired nursing care facility. It provides care for 123 patients in both skilled and intermediate care wings making it the largest single nursing home in the Presbyterian Homes, Inc. Sycamore Manor brought the total number of nursing care patients over 300—nearly double the number in residential care facilities and solidly establishing Presbyterian Homes, Inc., as a provider of nursing care in Pennsylvania.

Sycamore Manor Health Center is located just three miles from Williamsport Presbyterian Home. Although these sister facilities do not constitute a continuing care campus, their proximity assures residents of Williamsport Presbyterian Home a nearby nursing care facility should they need such care.

A garden patio placed at the center of the facility provides recreation and shared activity area for patients at Sycamore Manor Health Center.

Westminster Village

# Lehigh Manor
## (Westminster Village)
## 803 North Wahneta Street
## Allentown, Pennsylvania
## 1973-
# A Continuing Care Campus

Lehigh Manor, now known as Westminster Village, was originally built in 1966 as a for-profit nursing home known as Central Park Nursing Home. When acquired by Presbyterian Homes, Inc., the facility housed 127 nursing patients. The building was renovated to provide 98 nursing care beds and 10 residential care rooms.

Lehigh Manor became a continuing care campus in 1983 with the addition of an adjoining building with 42 independent living apartments known as Westminster House.

Westminster Village leads all the homes in the number of hours donated by their volunteers. In an innovative program developed in 1984, residents use an occupational therapy kitchen as part of rehabilitation therapy for patients at the facility. Nellie Lewis provided seed money toward the purchase of Lehigh Manor through a gift to Presbyterian Homes, Inc. The acquisition of Lehigh Manor put the corporation's nursing bed capacity well above its residential care capacity for the first time in its 45-year history.

# Nonprofit Services Associates (Nonprofit Services Associates, Inc.) 1217 Slate Hill Road Camp Hill, Pennsylvania 1975- The Consulting and Management Arm of Presbyterian Homes, Inc.

Nonprofit Services Associates was organized in 1975 to use the collective expertise of the administrative staff of Presbyterian Homes, Inc., in consulting work for subsidiary corporations and for facilities outside of Presbyterian Homes, Inc.

At this writing, the primary, on-going activities of N.S.A. provide management and data processing support for Presbyterian Apartments, Inc., a subsidiary corporation of Presbyterian Homes, Inc. N.S.A. also provides data processing support and management consulting for Huntingdon County Nursing Home, Huntingdon, and One West Penn, Carlisle.

N.S.A. has also done management consulting work for other non-profit homes for the aging in Pennsylvania and in Maryland. While not a large part of the total ministry of Presbyterian Homes, Inc., the consulting work has given key staff members experience in the operation of homes with different philosophies and management styles than their own. This varied experience benefits all the facilities in the Presbyterian Homes, Inc., system.

The Swaim Health Center

# Swaim Health Center
# Big Spring Road
# Newville, Pennsylvania
# 1977-
# A Nursing Home

Swaim Health Center opened in 1977, provided nursing care for 49 persons and was later expanded to its present capacity of 63 beds. The facility was the first expansion on the Parker Farm since the building of The Manor (residential home) which opened in January of 1941. The home was named for William T. Swaim, Jr., the first full-time administrator of Presbyterian Homes, Inc. Swaim gave the dedicatory address at the facility's opening.

This nursing facility along with the cottages that opened the following year and apartments the preceding year constituted the first operating continuing care campus owned by Presbyterian Homes, Inc. The first administrator of Swaim Health Center, John H. Earwood, was also the first of many graduate interns trained at corporate facilities. Earwood came to Presbyterian Homes, Inc., to complete the requirements for a master's degree in health care administration from North Texas State University.

Oxford Manor — Steward Home

# Oxford Manor-
# The Steward Home
# 7 Locust Street
# Oxford, Pennsylvania
# 1977-
# A Continuing Care Campus

Oxford Manor-The Steward Home is the current proper name for four different facilities that share one tract of land. And the tract of land has a name of its own.

The property is a 13-acre tract of land with a large stone mansion located near the center of Oxford donated by the Ware family. The first use of the property was a renovation of the original "Woods" mansion into apartments called Ware Presbyterian Village.

Oxford Manor and The Steward Home are separate wings of the same building connected by a commons area. The facility opened in 1977. Its west wing is a 40-unit residential care facility known as The Steward Home. Oxford Manor is a 100-bed nursing facility that occupies the rest of the building. On the same property are The Woods Apartments and The Woods Cottages. The first apartments are open at this writing and construction is underway at the Woods Cottages.

The names, though confusing, recognize the contributors that made the project possible. John Ware, III, donated the land. Dr. N.B. Steward made a bequest of several million dollars that provided much of the financing for the home that bears his name.

Stephen Proctor, presently vice president of operations of Presbyterian Homes, Inc., was the organizing administrator of the facility.

The Cathcart Health Center

Hutchinson House

# Cathcart Home/ Hutchinson House 445 Valley Forge Road Devon, Pennsylvania 1978- A Continuing Care Campus

The Eliza Cathcart Home opened on November 13, 1893, as a home for convalescents under the management of The Presbyterian Hospital, Philadelphia. The original home is a huge stone mansion which served for more than 80 years as a 47-bed nursing facility. Presbyterian Homes, Inc., acquired the original building from the trustees of the Stroud Estate, Philadelphia.

Beginning in 1978, Presbyterian Homes, Inc., planned to renovate the existing structure. The final plan adopted added a wing to the existing building with 63 nursing beds and eight apartments. The wing opened in 1983. The original building was then renovated to make 24 additional apartments which opened in 1984 for a total of 32. The apartments in the old stone structure follow all the contours of the original structure making each apartment noticably different than every other one.

Green Hall Apartments

Pine Circle Cottages

# Green Ridge Village
# Big Spring Road
# Newville, Pennsylvania
# 1978-
# A Continuing Care Campus

Most offices have plaques or pictures on the wall. In the administrator's office in Green Ridge Village most of the wall space is covered with large blueprints. Colored pins mark Cottages under construction, cottages completed, and proposed sites for roads and cottages to expand the Green Ridge Village Health Care Complex even further.

Other facilities on the Green Ridge Village continuing care campus include the original Parker Home, now used as a medical center and guest house; Manor Presbyterian Home, a residential home; and Swaim Health Center, a nursing home. Together, these facilities comprise the largest single unit of Presbyterian Homes, Inc., and, of course, the oldest.

Much of the land that supported sheep, corn, and alfalfa in the early days of the homes now supports new cottages and apartments. Of course, much open ground still remains both on the Parker land that belongs to the homes and on neighboring farms. And most of the land will be developed in the coming decade while preserving the pastoral atmosphere of the area.

Mr. and Mrs. Jack Poorman, residents of the Green Ridge Village community, both named the facility and set up the first trust fund for the endowment of benevolent care at Green Ridge Village.

Indiana Presbyterian Home

# Indiana Presbyterian Home
# 1155 Indian Springs Road
# Indiana, Pennsylvania
# 1983-
# A Nursing Home

Indiana Presbyterian Home opened in 1983. It is a 120-bed nursing care facility and the newest of the homes. With the opening of this home, Presbyterian Homes, Inc., reached a total capacity of more than 600 nursing care beds in seven facilities. Building in Kiskiminetas Presbytery completed a twelve-year cycle of buying or building nursing homes near or on the sites where residential homes were built in decades past. Indiana Presbyterian Home is less than 30 miles from Kittanning Presbyterian Home.

The home was built on a 7-acre tract of farmland donated by Julia Wilson Pound. Indiana Presbyterian Home quickly established a nursing, dietary, and recreational intern program for students from nearby Indiana University of Pennsylvania.

Community Home-Care Services

# Community Home-Care Services
# 1217 Slate Hill Road
# Camp Hill, Pennsylvania
# 1984-
# Health care services for
# those living at home

Community Home-Care Services is the newest ministry of Presbyterian Homes, Inc. The program is administered from the Camp Hill offices of the corporation by June Hoffman, R.N., director—formerly the director of nursing care services at Oxford Manor. Community Home-Care Services offers people with both temporary and chronic health problems the care they need to remain at home. Most home health care services are routine—help with house-keeping, help with medical appliances, changing dressings for people unable to do it themselves, and similar tasks—but for those suffering chronic and partially incapacitating illnesses, help with routine chores means the difference between extended hospitalization, and returning to their own homes.

The work of Community Home-Care Services nurses, nurse aides, and home companions is as varied as the illnesses and injuries and ages of their patients:

—a stroke victim with some memory loss and confusion living at home with her husband of forty years.

—a couple stricken with diabetes living in retirement apartments.

—a young woman left a paraplegic after a swimming accident.

—an older couple caring for an aged parent with Alzheimer's disease.

At this writing, Community Home-Care Services operates five offices. They are located in Harrisburg, Carlisle, Williamsport, and Oxford in Pennsylvania, as well as in Wheeling, West Virginia.

Mark H. Kennedy

# Mark H. Kennedy Park St. Clairsville, Ohio 1985- Cottages and Studio Apartments for the Aging

At this writing Mark H. Kennedy Park is under construction with several model apartments and a common building slated for completion this year. When completed this facility will be the first unit of Presbyterian Homes, Inc., outside of Pennsylvania. The facility is located in Upper Ohio Valley Presbytery which includes southeastern Ohio and the northwest corner of West Virginia. Mark H. Kennedy Park will offer its residents independent retirement living in studio, one bedroom, and two bedroom cottages and apartments.

A newly opened office of Community Home-Care Services in nearby Wheeling, West Virginia, will provide home health care services for residents who need such services in the future.

As is evident from the name, the site of the new community has been made available through the vision and generosity of Mark H. Kennedy, a long-time St. Clairsville resident.

The Woods Cottages

# The Woods Cottages
# 7 Locust Street
# Oxford, Pennsylvania
# 1985
# Cottages for the Aging

Woods Cottages will be built on the grounds of Oxford Manor-The Steward Home. The cottages are one- and two-bedroom bungalows designed for older couples who want independent living in a secure environment. The cottages will be similar to the cottages built at Green Ridge Village. With the addition of the Woods Cottages Oxford Manor will offer every level of care from the independent living of the Woods Cottages, to resident care in The Steward Home, to skilled nursing in the Oxford Manor.

One unit of the Presbyterian Homes new Community Home-Care Services operates from Oxford Manor and will serve the medical needs of Woods Cottages residents which do not require institutional care.

# Courtland Manor
# Salisbury and College Roads
# Dover, Delaware
# (1986-)
# (Purchased in 1984)
# A Nursing Home

Although not yet operated by Presbyterian Homes, Inc., (the home will operate by the corporation in late 1986) Courtland Manor was purchased in 1984. When Presbyterian Homes, Inc., begins operation of Courtland Manor, the facility will be the first nursing care facility operated by the corporation outside of Pennsylvania.

At the time this facility opens, Mark H. Kennedy Park in Ohio will be partially occupied and the Wheeling, West Virginia office of Community Home-Care Services will have been open for a year. The beginning of 1985 saw the corporation operating in one state; the end of 1986 will see corporate facilities operating in at least four states.

Courtland Manor lies northwest of Dover's central business district. Its 17-acre grounds adjoin a residential subdivision and the campus of Delaware State College.

This latest unit of Presbyterian Homes, Inc., will raise the total capacity of the various facilities to nearly 800 nursing care beds in eight nursing homes; more than 600 apartments and semi-detached houses in three subsidiary apartment complexes, four continuing care campuses, and a retirement community under development in Ohio; and 127 residential care rooms in six facilities. Depending on the speed with which present projects are completed and are occupied, the total number of persons living in Presbyterian Homes, Inc., facilities will approach 2,000 persons when operation of Courtland Manor is initiated in 1986.

William T. Swaim, Jr.—Albert Schartner

# APPENDIX IV.

This section includes brief biographies of the two men who served as the chief executives of Presbyterian Homes, Inc., since 1940. In that year William T. Swaim, Jr., was named the first full-time administrator of the corporation. For the six years that preceded his appointment, Swaim served as part-time administrator. During the period from 1928 through 1934, the day- to-day administration of the corporation was handled by the executive committee of the board of trustees.

Swaim's full term of service extended roughly from his appointment as a trustee of the corporation on May 2, 1933, through the last day of December of 1969.

Albert L. Schartner joined the corporation as assistant administrator on July 1, 1964. On January 1, 1970, he was appointed administrator, succeeding Bill Swaim and becoming the second administrator in the coporation's history. A realignment of the board of trustees in 1977 expanded the duties of the administrator. The president of the board became the chairman of the board. The administrator (then executive vice president) was made president and chief executive officer of the corporation and given the executive responsibilities of president in addition to the responsibilities that previously constituted the administrator's work.

Both men have made Presbyterian Homes, Inc., their life's work. The brief essays that follow will introduce them.

## The Rev. William T. Swaim, Jr. Presbyterian Apartments Harrisburg, PA

The Reverend William T. "Bill" Swaim, Jr., was born in Selma, Alabama, on November 5, 1906—a town which Bill admits is more famous for Civil Rights protests in the 1960s than for his birth. Swaim said his boyhood was typical for children growing up in the American South. His main activity for fun and in games was jumping—jumping

169

over fences, jumping across ditches, jumping into water, and playing all sorts of leapfrog games.

Jumping around was also a big part of Swaim's family life. By the time Bill was six, his family had moved to Missouri, back to Alabama, to Tennessee and then to Memphis, Texas, where Bill spent his grade school years. Bill's father was a pastor in the Evangelical Presbyterian Church. His ministry took the family to churches in several states throughout the South and the Midwest and finally to Pennsylvania where Bill Swaim eventually made his home.

Bill was the second of three children—three boys. All three boys became ordained ministers. Bill's older brother, Richard Carter Swaim, was a translator of high reputation who was in charge of the translation of The Revised Standard Version of the Bible. Each of the Swaim brothers eventually embraced the tenets of the liberal wing of the church. Their father preached in the Hell-fire and brimstone tradition of Billy Sunday and Robert Jones, Sr. — father of the very controversial Bob Jones, Jr. — head of the segregated Christian College of the same name.

Swaim also jumped through three different colleges and earned as many degrees before becoming an ordained minister in the Presbyterian Church. With his ordination, Swaim was on his way to realizing his boyhood goal of spreading the Gospel from the pulpit. On the way to his ordination, Swaim earned three degrees — a bachelor of arts degree from the University of Tennessee, and both a bachelor and a master of divinity degree (STB abd STM) from Western Seminary, now Pittsburgh Theological Seminary.

In April of 1933 Swaim was named pastor of the Big Springs Presbyterian Church in Newville and within a month was elected to the board of trustees of Presbyterian Home of Central Pennsylvania. With the same energy and application Swaim brought to everything he did in life, Swaim got involved in the operations of the Home. He was quickly elected acting secretary of the board and began getting involved in the daily operations of the homes.

In 1940 Swaim was named the first full-time administrator of Presbyterian Home of Central Pennsylvania, although from the first year, people involved with the daily operations of the Homes—applicants for residence, applicants for jobs, vendors, suppliers, contributors, and those with complaints big and small—knew Bill Swaim was the man to see.

Until his resignation as President of the Homes in late 1969, Swaim's life and activities revolved around his work. He was elected a District Governor of Rotary International shortly after World War II. Whenever he traveled for Rotary, he would make contacts that benefitted the Homes. Beginning in 1957 Swaim taught courses—"Short Courses" he called them—on administering Homes for the Aging. The courses Swaim taught helped to give the Homes a national reputation since they attracted students from around the country. They also introduced Swaim to potential supervisors for the several homes he administered.

During the 1960s eye surgery and ill-advised surgery on his hands slowed Swaim down and, in part, led to his retirement on the last day of December of 1969. At his retirement, Swaim left the Homes to his assistant, now President and Chief Executive Officer, the Rev. Albert Schartner, to work on local history projects. One of the principles Swaim taught in his short courses was that the former—especially retired—administrator should gracefully and quickly get out of the way of his successor. Swaim did.

Since his retirement, Bill Swaim helped to organize the Tri- Centennial celebrations of two Presbyterian Churches in the Newville area, has published dozens of articles on the history of the Newville-Carlisle area, and has an ever-growing list of speeches he has and will deliver on various aspects of local history.

Swaim's "retirement" days begin at 5 a.m. He goes to the second floor lobby of Presbyterian Apartments where he and his wife, Alice, have lived since Bill's retirement. He writes and reads until lunch, then runs errands or visits or travels to libraries, or continues with any of a hundred projects that fill his always- busy life. The evening will often find Swaim attending a meeting or delivering a speech to a historical society or service club. Seven decades have not slowed his walking pace either—a brisk stride that carries him along nearly twice as fast as the rest of the people on the sidewalks of Harrisburg.

The Swaim pace pulled Presbyterian Homes of Central Pennsylvania along from caring for ten women when Swaim was named to the board to more than 175 residents in homes and 200 more in apartments at his retirement. In addition to his work for the Homes, Swaim was instrumental in founding both the American Association of Homes for the Aging (AAHA) and the Pennsylvania Association of Non-Profit Homes for the Aging (PANPHA).

Bill and Alice Swaim are the parents of two daughters, Elizabeth and Kathie. Both are college professors. Alice MacKenzie Swaim has published several books of poems and has had her poems published in national magazines and in leading newspapers. **The Rev. Albert L. Schartner** 304 North Baltimore Street Dillsburg, PA

On July 18, 1931, Albert Lyman Schartner was born on a small family farm in rural Rhode Island. He lived on the farm until he was eight-years-old. His mother died when he was just a year old and his father died seven years later. After his father's death, he was adopted and raised by an aunt and uncle living in his grandparent's home in rural Massachusetts.

Young Schartner was raised as an only child. There were few children around. In the early years in Rhode Island, the nearest neighbor was a county home for the aging. Later, growing up on the edge of a small town with three aunts, two uncles, and grandparents, Schartner was always comfortable around older people.

During his high school years, Schartner leaned toward law as a career, but most of his friends and most of his social activities were related to the church he attended—a small United Presbyterian Church in Massachusetts. He majored in English at Boston University for the first two years of his college training, but left that school for Westminster College in western Pennsylvania at the start of his junior year. "I was student number 5735 at BU and I didn't like being a number," Schartner said of his first two years as an undergraduate.

At Westminster, a Presbyterian College, Schartner decided to go to seminary and enter the ministry. Schartner says he has a firm conviction of God's guidance in his life.

After Seminary and further graduate study in Europe, Schartner was called to be pastor of a Presbyterian Church in Irwin, Pennsylvania. The church had recently split over doctrinal issues, the congregation was divided, and an unfinished building program was stalled.

Schartner applied himself to rebuilding the congregation and to restoring unity. The congregation grew together and the church began to grow. At the end of seven years, Schatner was preaching two services on Sunday mornings and two recently completed- additions to the building were already proving too small for the needs of the congregation which had increased ten times in membership. At that time Schartner was receiving persistent offers to pastor still larger congregations.

While such offers were tempting, Schartner enjoyed administration and wanted to work in care for the aging. He spent several of the vacations he had from his pastoral work taking courses in health care administration and working with the aging. He was also gently prodded by Frank Magor, Executive of the Pittsburgh Presbytery, to seek a position in care for the aging.

At Magor's suggestion, Bill Swaim came to Irwin to meet Schartner and decided the same day that Schartner was the man Presbyterian Homes of Central Pennsylvania needed. Later that month, Schartner and his wife Kathleen drove to Dillsburg to consider the offer and to meet the trustees. Schartner was named assistant administrator by the board several weeks later.

On July 1, 1964, Schartner reported for his first day of work in the one-room office of Presbyterian Homes of Central Pennsylvania. Any job change involves transition, but for Schartner, the change was dramatic.

At Irwin, Schartner was surrounded by people and always busy meeting and counseling his growing congregation. After the bustle of a growing pastorate, Schartner spent the first week of his new job reading the files of the corporation. He questioned his choice. Maybe he had chosen wrongly, the back area of a cramped office was not the work he imagined.

According to Schartner and his new boss Bill Swaim, the doubts ended the next week. Schartner started a round of visits to all the homes beginning with a visit to The Schock Home in Mount Joy. The resident who answered the door, a small woman whose face Schartner described as radiant, welcomed him and his vocation was confirmed. The residents and the staff insisted the new administrator bring his family back for dinner on the following Sunday. The dinner concluded with an ice cream sundae bar the staff made up for the Schartners' two young sons.

Shortly after Schartner's introduction to the several homes, he began case work with applicants and with new residents. His first case was a woman living alone in Chester County who had been recommended for immediate guest-ship by her pastor. The woman barely existed on a meager pension. For weeks she lived on peanut butter and crackers. Schartner worked quickly, clearing up all the paperwork and getting the woman in the first vacancy, which turned out to be the local home in Kennett Square. In the weeks that followed, the woman's health was restored. Schartner soon took over all of the case work for the corporation as well as secretaryship of the board of trustees.

Schartner performed most of the office work during the next five years, while Bill Swaim concentrated on building programs and public relations. The division of labor gave Schartner full command of both the scope of the work and of the details of day-to-day operations. When Swaim retired in 1969, Schartner was ready to lead the corporation. He had worked out a program for expanding the corporation along very different lines than was true of the past forty years.

Under his leadership, the corporation has grown from 175 guests in nine homes, plus 200 more in apartments, with a staff of forty and an annual budget of $300,000 to serving 1,500 persons in several types of facilities with a staff of 900 and an annual budget of $28,000,000. The corporation provides every level of care from independent living to skilled nursing care, as well as day care services, home health care services, and various community services in 20 locations in Pennsylvania, Delaware, Ohio, and West Virginia.

Schartner earned a bachelor of arts degree from Westminster College, and both master of divinity and master of theology degrees from Pittsburgh Theological Seminary. In 1979 he completed a master of arts degree in health care administration from North Texas State University.

He is a member of several state and national groups concerned with the care of the aging—including past president of Pennsylvania Association of Non-Profit Homes for the Aging (PANPHA) and past executive board member of the American Association of Homes for the Aging. He is a past president of the Carlisle Rotary Club and his area Board of Education. He was recently awarded the distinguished Service Award by PANPHA and is currently president of Presbyterian Association of Homes for the Aging.

Albert Schartner and his wife Kathleen live in Dillsburg. They have three children: Dale, who is an auditor with Blue Cross of Western Pennsylvania; Carl, who is employed with the Pittsburgh office of Arthur Anderson in health care consulting; and Beth Anne, who is a junior at Beaver College near Philadelphia.

Nurturing the Young.

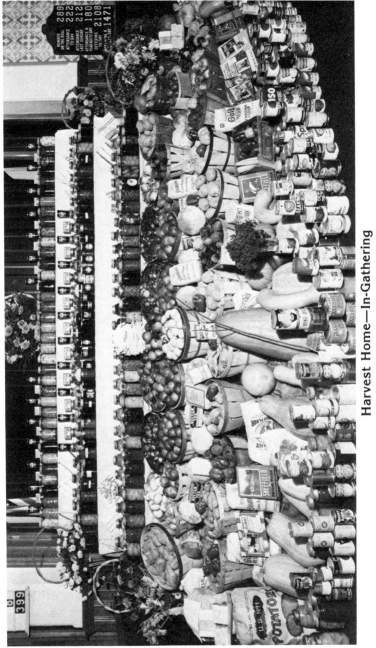

Harvest Home—In-Gathering

# The growing services of Presbyterian Homes, Inc.

## Serving most of Pennsylvania and the Upper Ohio Valley Presbytery Area of West Virginia and Ohio

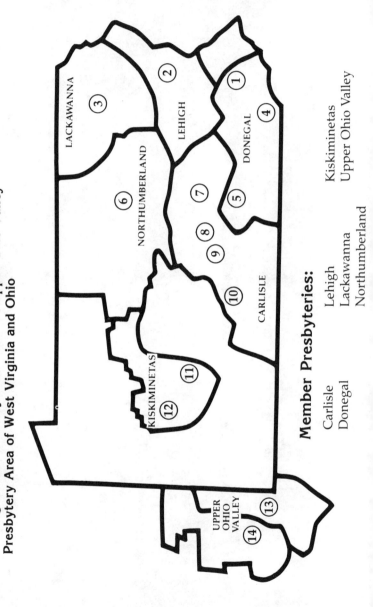

## Member Presbyteries:

| | | |
|---|---|---|
| Carlisle | Lehigh | Kiskiminetas |
| Donegal | Lackawanna | Upper Ohio Valley |
| | Northumberland | |

178

# Presbyterian Homes Facilities

1. **Devon, PA**
   Eliza Cathcart Home
   Cathcart Health Center
   Hutchinson House,
   independent living

2. **Allentown, PA**
   Westminster Village
   Westminster House,
   independent living
   Westminster Health Center

3. **Scranton, PA**
   Geneva House, independent
   living

4. **Oxford, PA**
   Oxford Manor
   Oxford Manor Health Center
   N. B. Steward Home,
   residential
   The Woods, independent
   living
   Community Home-Care
   Services
   Oxford Manor Day Care
   Center

5. **Mount Joy, PA**
   Schock Presbyterian Home,
   residential
   Meals on Wheels

6. **Williamsport/Montoursville, PA**
   Williamsport Presbyterian Home,
   residential
   Sycamore Manor Health Center
   Community Home-Care
   Services

7. **Harrisburg, PA**
   Presbyterian Apartments
   Community Home-Care
   Services

8. **Camp Hill, PA**
   Presbyterian Homes, Inc.
   Administrative Offices
   Community Home-Care
   Services, Administrative Offices
   Nonprofit Service Associates,
   Inc.

9. **Carlisle, PA**
   Carlisle Presbyterian Home,
   residential
   Forest Park Health Center
   Community Home-Care
   Services
   Meals on Wheels

10. **Newville, PA**
    Green Ridge Village
    Independent living apartments
    and cottages
    Swaim Health Center
    Manor Home, residential
    Parker House, Guest House,
    Medical Office
    Meals on Wheels

11. **Indiana, PA**
    Indiana Presbyterian Home,
    nursing

12. **Kittanning, PA**
    Kittanning Presbyterian Home,
    residential

13. **Wheeling, WV**
    Community Home-Care
    Services

14. **St. Clairsville, OH**
    Mark H. Kennedy Park
    A developing retirement
    community

**Educational Programs and Interpretation Displays
available to Churches, Community Groups and others.**

Caring and Sharing

# About the Author

Neil G. Gussman

**Neil G. Gussman** is a copy writer, news writer, and researcher. He is currently a master's degree candidate in the American Studies program at The Pennsylvania State University.